MARXISM IN CHINA

Marxism in China

Su Shaozhi
Wu Dakun
Ru Xin
Cheng Renqian

with a foreword by
Ken Coates

SPOKESMAN

First published in 1983
by Spokesman
Bertrand Russell House
Gamble Street
Nottingham NG7 4ET

Tel. 0602 708318

British Library Cataloguing in Publication Data

Shaozhi, Su
  Marxism in China.
  1. Communism — Great Britain
   I. Title
   335.4'0951   HX418.5

ISBN 0 85124 374 6

This book is copyright under the Berne Convention. All rights are strictly reserved. No part of this publication may be reproduced or transmitted in any form or by any means without permission.

Copyright © Spokesman, 1983

Printed by the Russell Press Ltd., Nottingham.

Contents

	Foreword *by Ken Coates*	7
I	Developing Marxism under Contemporary Conditions *Su Shaozhi*	13
II	The Asiatic Mode of Production in History as Viewed by Political Economy in Its Broad Sense *Wu Dakun*	53
III	Is Humanism Revisionism? *Ru Xin*	78
IV	Some Questions on the Reassessment of Rosa Luxemburg *Cheng Renqian*	96
	The Contributors	124

Foreword

China has been the subject of considerable discussion in the Western press, as various political and social policies have changed since the cultural revolution. Western socialists also have engaged in controversies about the meaning of the new economic reforms in China, and about the effects of changes in Chinese foreign policy. The practical political prescriptions of the Chinese Communist Party, so embodied, have provoked debate among both opponents and supporters in all Western countries. But the development of the underlying thought of the Chinese Communists has been strangely ignored, as if the turbulent flux of events in this crucial nation had no mental reflections.

In fact, there has begun an extraordinary renaissance of socialist ideas during the post-Mao years. After years of isolation the Chinese have now launched into publishing an extensive selection of writings by theorists who hitherto were quite unavailable in their country. Writings from the heroic period of the Russian revolution, long suppressed in the USSR itself, now begin to appear in print in Beijing. Several volumes of Bukharin have been published, alongside other heretical texts, with which it becomes possible to form a more objective picture of the evolution of socialist thought not only in Russia but also wherever the Russian influence for evil or good has been felt. The ghosts of Bukharin and Preobrazhensky have been silently haunting (and sometimes actively intervening) in the practical policy debates of every developing country which has experimented with socialist planning in recent years.

When I reported on the fact that such texts were now available to the Chinese political cadres, one well-known scholar asked me, with an indulgent smile, whether I did not think that more contemporary figures might also be worthy of publication. Of course I do. Indeed, the Chinese publishing programme begins to extend to include a number of authors whose works are not available, say, in the USSR.

What my Western professor failed to understand when he questioned the contemporary relevance of such long-dead Communist scholars as Bukharin was the extent to which their voices are necessary to the recovery of a full socialist theory. They are necessary, not because they were "right" where their victorious opponents had been "wrong". Protagonists in political disputes are by no means always completely justified or unjustified. Real political thought, and indeed, all valid social analysis, proceeds in a dialectic which arrives at truth through conflict. But in such conflict we cannot normally fix the moment of arrival at a particular instant. True, there are nodal points at which we may conclude, after the event, that great issues have been resolved. But even arrival at these junctures does not cancel the lessons of the debates leading up to them, or prevent "defeated" ideas from re-emerging at a later time, after "victorious" ones have been tried out.

Where political debates have been resolved by arbitrary decisions, one may be excused for believing that such resolution is even more likely to be flawed and historically limited. For these reasons, the recovery of the past can have an importance which is anything but academic, and is by no means restricted to the possibility of re-writing history. In societies in which history is undervalued there may be a surfeit of contradictory accounts of any particular event, so that even scholars may sometimes fail to appreciate the overwhelming importance of open access to the historical record. Where one encounters the suppression of that record, and officially imposed amnesia, there one necessarily enters an arena of irrationality. To leave that arena is to restore the possibility of objective thought, not only in the schoolroom, but also in many fields of practical endeavour.

A socialist movement which seeks to annul its own past must thereby jeopardize its future. A small legion of modern writers on development and under-development will make greater or lesser sense in a context in which educated opinion has free recall of the momentous controversies of the socialist movement, than they would in a sheltered environment which lacked this formative exposure.

Su Shaozhi, in his paper commemorating the Marx Centenary, warns his colleagues against trying to "answer . . . questions simply by citing some relevant passages from classical Marx writings". He lists a number of crises in the world communist movement which have "put a series of sharp questions before Marxism, which we should never evade". The papers in this book are an evidence that Chinese Marxists are indeed facing a number of questions which are still evaded by communist leaderships in many parts of the world.

Wu Dakun addresses the problem of the Asiatic Mode of Production, which was an important Marxian category, not only in *The Critique of Political Economy*, but in *Capital* itself and indeed throughout the works of both Marx and Engels. In an attempt to vindicate the unilinear theory of evolution, Stalin "abolished" this category, as Professor Wu Dakun explains. Its recovery in the West was part of the theoretical spoils of the annulment of the Stalin cult, and was greatly reinforced by the publication of Marx' *Grundrisse* in most western languages. It will assuredly help the development of historical studies in China, but it may also have an analytical importance in helping us to understand the contemporary evolution of the Soviet Union as well as China. Professor Wu Dakun rightly dismisses the work of Wittfogel, which is an indefensible misuse of the category. Wittfogel began his academic life as a Communist scholar, and there are notable discrepancies between his early writings and his later propaganda during the epoch of the cold war, when he sought to explain the modern world in terms of conflict between Western democracy and oriental despotism.[1]

Rudolf Bahro, whose stimulating commentary on "actually existing socialisms", *The Alternative*, not yet published, makes a different use of the concept, and it will be most interesting to read the Chinese response to Bahro's views.

Ru Xin rehabilitates a good deal more than the thoughts of the young Marx in his essay on Humanism. This is an eloquent text, which speaks for itself. Mr. Ru Xin is the vice-president of the Chinese Academy of Social Sciences. His work will help to restore to his countrymen a fully rounded picture of the real Marx, whose youthful ideas were developed, but never lost in his mature work.

Finally, this collection of papers includes the most stimulating assessment of Rosa Luxemburg by Cheng Renqian. Luxemburg is another historical figure whose importance can hardly be over-estimated. That she should be the object of serious consideration in modern China is itself an important political development.

To my mind, the theory of socialist democracy is still

inadequate, just as its practice leaves a great space for further development. Contrary to the opinions of ideologues in the West, democracy cannot be equated with freedom, but it does constitute an indispensible condition for the development of freedom. It is impossible to conceive of the overcoming of human exploitation without the development of ever more profound democratic structures, civil freedoms, and institutions of popular accountability. Luxemburg offers a most valuable point of departure for this work, and all of us will wish the Chinese people well in their further development of the insights so clearly spelt out by Professor Cheng in this paper.

Socialism is an international force, and the need for the most thorough-going international commitment is strongly reinforced by the crisis in which the modern world of capital is toiling. World economic crisis has historically been resolved in war. War today would result in such horrendous destruction as would place the future of civilisation itself in jeopardy. For this reason, it is urgently necessary that the socialists in all countries should come closer together, and that they should be able to share their ideas in the most fraternal and honest exchanges.

It is in this cause that we offer this small selection of writings by our Chinese friends, as a contribution to what we hope will be a dialogue which can knit us all more closely together.

Ken Coates

Footnote
1. Karl A. Wittfogel is best known for his *Oriental Despotism*, first published in 1957. This work was taken up and widely publicised, because it was entirely consonant with various cold war prejudices. But Wittfogel's earlier writings closely followed Marxian categories, even though they were to fall under unrestrained condemnation by the Soviet leadership during the 1930s. The Chinese Communists seem to have

rejected the concept of an Asiatic mode of production as long ago as 1928. But British Marxism did not follow either the Chinese or the Soviet teaching in this respect, and Emile Burns, Gordon Childe and R.P. Dutt all made use of Marx's writings on Asiatic society right through the decade of the '30s, and even as late as 1942. Wittfogel's earlier analysis was published in 1931 under the title *Wirtschaft und Gesellschaft Chinas*. An English summary was published in the journal *Zeitschrift fur Sozialforschung*, IV: 26-60 under the title *The Foundations and Stages of Chinese Economic History*. Unlike the argument in *Oriental Despotism*, which was presented as a "comparative study of total power", this earlier work was constrained by scientific parameters and entered a detailed discussion as to whether certain phases of Chinese society might properly be described as "feudal". All these nuances are missing from the cold war diatribe of Wittfogel's later years.

I

Developing Marxism Under Contemporary Conditions

In Commemoration of the Centenary of the Death of Karl Marx

Su Shaozhi

I. Marxism must keep developing, or it will become lifeless

One hundred years ago, that is, shortly after Marx's death in March 1883, his student and comrade-in-arms Wilhelm Liebknecht said in a speech at his graveside: "He never dies. He lives in the *hearts* of the proletarians, in the *minds* of the proletarians. His name is immortal, and his theories will keep developing." The entire world history of the past hundred years has proved what foresight and sagacity are contained in this statement.

Reviewing the history of the previous century and more, we are gratified to note the great victory of world historic significance gained by Marxism. At its very inception, Marxism was but one of the many schools of thought concerning the theory of socialism-communism. To quote Engels, "Working men of all countries, unite! But few voices responded when we proclaimed these words to the world forty-two years ago. (i.e. at the time of the publication of *The Communist Manifesto*), on the eve of the first Paris Revolution in which the proletariat came out with demands of its own."[1] Before long, however, Marx's theory triumphed over the opposing ideological systems of all descriptions and became the guiding ideology of the international proletarian revolutionary movement. One-third of a century following the death of Marx, the success of the October Revolution, led by the great Lenin, transformed, for the first time in human history, Marx's theory of scientific socialism into reality. After World War II, a number of other countries took the roads of socialism. Irrespective of how the subsequent historical events in some countries should be appraised, the establishment of the socialist system in the Soviet Union and a number of other countries should be regarded as breaking, by the proletarian revolution, the weak links of the chain of the imperialist world of the time.

The victory of the Chinese revolution, led by the Communist Party of China, gave rise to the socialist system in a big oriental country with a history of several thousand years and a population amounting to one quarter of the world's total. This is a fruitful result of the integration of the universal truth of Marxism with the concrete practice of the Chinese revolution. With the emergence of socialist China and with the embarking of some other Third World countries on the socialist road, the "spectre" of communism formerly haunting Europe has now appeared on the broad horizon of different continents.

In keeping with its becoming a powerful force in world politics, Marxism has grown into a formidable tide in the ideological and cultural spheres of the contemporary world. People cannot forget that, when Marx's *Capital* made its debut, the capitalist world tried to choke it with sheer silence. Today, however, there is no civilised country which does not publish some title or other of Marx's works, which does not have some kind of institute for studies of Marxism, and which does not have a certain number of scholars doing theoretical studies under the banner of Marxism; there is no university of any reputation in the world which does not offer some specialisation or lectures on Marxism; and there are no serious works in the social sciences or the humanities which can completely evade touching on the momentous problems raised by Marxism.

At the 16th World Philosophical Symposium held in Düsseldorf, West Germany, in August 1978 to discuss the central theme of "philosophy and world outlook in modern science", President Walter Scheel of the host country said in his opening speech;

> As a matter of fact, in the thirty years of my political career, everyday I come into contact with Marx this or that way... It is true that today there are still disciples of J. G. Fichte. But no political activities can be carried on in the name of Fichte. On the other hand, Marx's thinking is exercising an influence over the life of billions of people. And this not only in socialist countries. Why has Marx such universal influence? In my view, it is because he concentrated his energies on studying the most pressing problem, namely, the social problem of his time. Even today this remains the most pressing problem concerning millions upon millions of people. Marxism will continue to exist at least until there is a solution of the social problems on a world scale.

The above comment by a non-Marxist proves from another angle that, since Marx's departure from this world of ours, the theories he expounded and the social movement he initiated have become an intellectual entity and a vigorous political reality commanding the attention of everybody.

None the less, while commemorating the centenary of Marx's death, all serious-minded Marxists cannot afford to be carried away by the successes already achieved, but should rather resolve to devote their main effort to tackling the difficulties and problems before them. We cannot but face up to the internationally current contentions that "Marxism has become outmoded" and that "Marxism is now in crisis", and to the indifferent attitude shown by a number of people in China towards Marxism. The argument that "Marxism has become outmoded" is being pushed mainly by bourgeois scholars (inluding some "Western Marxists") who are exerting themselves to prove that either the Marxist thesis on capitalist economic relations, or the Marxist analysis of the superstructure of capitalist society, belongs to 19th century ideology and has thus become utterly out of keeping with contemporary conditions. Since the 1970s, the contention that "Marxism is now in crisis" has become fashionable in academic discussions among "Western Marxists" who argue that now Marxism is beset with a genuine "theoretical crisis" which "is set within the context of the crisis of contemporary capitalism and certain crisis situations in contemporary socialism".[2] And L. Althusser put it sharply like this; ". . . It is clear from many signs that today Marxism is once again in crisis, and that this crisis is an open one. Which means visible to everyone ... We are *living through* it, and have been for a long time."[3]

What should be our approach to these erroneous ideological trends and attitudes towards Marxism prevalent both in China and abroad? Of course, we should first of all make an analysis of the matter. As it is, the historical, social, political, partisan and cultural backgrounds of these trends and attitudes are highly complex and varied. Internationally, we can in a certain measure attribute the various ideological trends to class struggle. Some people in the West declare that "Marxism has become outmoded" and that "Marxism is now in crisis" because of traditional class prejudices and out of the requirements of ideological struggle. This analysis is, of course, correct. But *it is far from adequate*, for it shows only one aspect of the matter. We have to go a step further and explain the matter from a theoretical angle instead of brushing it aside with the simplified statement, fashionable in the past, that it is merely "vicious slander by the class enemy". We must note that, to a certain degree, the arguments that "Marxism has become outmoded" and that "Marxism is now in crisis", as well as the indifference towards Marxism, are a sort of punishment for the dogmatic attitude to Marxism. It cannot be denied that, for a time, there existed in the international communist movement and our own Party the erroneous tendency for dogmatizing Marxism and sanctifying the resolutions of the Third International and the Soviet experiences, and that, for a long period, there existed in the political life of our country and in its ideological sphere the personality cult and the erroneous "Left" tendency of a closed-door policy. All these seriously impeded the vigorous development of Marxism for a certain period of time so that it failed to make exploration of, and give answers to, the many new phenomena in the development of modern capitalism, the many new problems in the contemporary practice of socialism, the many new achievements in present-day natural sciences, and the many newborn disciplines of present-day social sciences — exploration and answers that are timely, theoretically profound and can withstand the test of experience itself. Just as Comrade Mao Zedong said, "Marxism must necessarily advance; it must develop along with practice and cannot stand still. It would become lifeless if it were stagnant and stereotyped."[4] Once a theory becomes incapable of answering the questions posed by life or the masses, it will inevitably be "cold-shouldered" by them, and its adversaries with varied motives of their own will seize the opportunity to make trouble. There is nothing strange about this at all.

While commemorating the centenary of the death of Marx, we must, out of the most serious sense of responsibility, put before ourselves and all those loyal to Marxism the task which should have been set out long ago, and this task is that we must study and answer the various problems raised by the present era.

So far as a great thinker and revolutionary teacher is concerned, there is no better way of commemorating him than by studying his thinking in real earnest and scientifically probing into the relationship between his thinking and contemporary reality. This is because his career is the process of the development of his great thinking itself, the process of such thinking playing its role — i.e., the process of a specific theory gripping the masses — in the course of history. In the final analysis, therefore, the best way for Chinese Marxists to commemorate such a great revolutionary forerunner as Marx is by persisting in and developing Marxism.

The relationship between persisting in something and developing it is dialectical; the two aspects form an inner unity and one should not be separated from the other. The basic tenets of Marxism are a scientific generalisation of the objective laws of historical development. Departure from this understanding as a prerequisite will lead the development of Marxism astray. Only by persisting in Marxism, therefore, can we develop it. On the other hand, the fundamental reason why Marx's theory is powerful and why it could attract to its banner thousands upon thousands of people ardently seeking truth is that it based itself on the latest developments of the socio-economic life of the time, absorbed the latest achievements of mankind's multi-disciplinary practice of the time and summarized the latest experiences of the proletariat's struggle of the time and thus solved the "historical enigma" with which people of the time were most concerned. *Marxism has vitality precisely because it continuously draws its life-force from the steadily developing reality.* To understand Marxism in line with this most fundamental characteristic, and to approach Marxism in line with its most receptive spirit, will forever preclude the problems of Marxism ever becoming "outmoded" or its ever being "in crisis", and will help eliminate the indifferent attitude to Marxism. Only by creatively developing Marxism will it be possible to really persist in Marxism.

To develop Marxism while persisting in it and vice versa, to ensure that our effort to develop Marxism does not swerve away from the broad path of the science of Marxism which has been verified by practice, and to use the developed Marxism to guide the practice under new historical conditions — such is our attitude to Marxism.

Ever since the discussion in China on taking practice as the criterion for verifying truth, more and more Chinese theoretical workers have taken to persisting in creative Marxism as their common principle. The Third Plenary Session of the Chinese Communist Party's Eleventh Central Committee held in December 1978 reaffirmed the Marxist ideological-political line and made it the guiding principle for the Party's ideological and theoretical work. Thus there is now the most favourable condition for our persisting in and developing Marxism. But this does not mean that such a correct principle has been thoroughly put into effect in China's theoretical circles. It should be admitted that the present situation in our theoretical circles falls somewhat short of the requirements of the principle of persisting in and developing Marxism. *We already have a correct principle, so what is essential now is to translate it into action* and use *the concrete acomplishments* in our theoretical studies to demonstrate the creativeness and invincibility of Marxism.

II. Marxists must face the contemporary world and answer the challenges posed to Marxists on the international scene

Now we have the task of persisting in and developing Marxism under conditions of the 1980s. What new phenomena, then, should be the main subjects of our studies? What new issues should we mainly solve? In other words, what challenges to Marxism should we strive to answer?

The challenges to Marxism on the international scene can be directly related to the rise of Western "Marxology" and "Western Marxism".

Prior to the late 1950s, the bourgeois theoreticians adopted an attitude of hypocritical indifference. From the 1960s onwards, however, the situation changed completely. A "Marx craze" began to appear in the West. Many scholars, including the chief exponents of some schools of thought, wrote books making textual research, interpretation and elaboration of Marx's works. Some of these scholars who are strict in their style of study have done certain significant work, while others, who study Marx's thinking for the definite purpose of ideological struggle, distort and criticize Marxism by interpreting Marx's writings in a manner all their own.

Unlike the Western "Marxologists" who openly declare their un-Marxist (or even anti-Marxist) stand, most of the "Western Marxists" announce that they are "genuine Marxists". Quite a few of them have even joined the Communist Parties in their own countries and some have really dedicated themselves to the struggle to transform the old world. Although "Western Marxism" has a much longer history than Western "Marxology", both began to thrive in the same period. In his pamphlet on the progress of social sciences since World War II, Daniel Bell wrote, "In the 1960s and 1970s, one saw a surprising upsurge of Marxist politics and neo-Marxist thought on a scale largely unexpected, following the sense of exhaustion of radical ideas in the West by the end of the 1950s."[5] The "Western Marxists" have launched prolonged, sharp and heated polemics on the most fundamental theses of Marxism. Some people figuratively describe these polemics as "Marx's Renaissance".

Although the challenges to Marxism on the international scene can be directly related to the rise of

Western "Marxology" and "Western Marxism", they have a deeper historical background. The various challenges in the international theoretical circles to Marxism are merely a theoretical expression of the new changes and developments of world economy, politics and social reality. Fundamentally speaking, they are due to the following factors:

1. The swift development of science and technology in the 20th century has had an enormous, profound and sustained influence on the various aspects of human material and spiritual life, thus considerably changing the face of the world.

2. A swift and marked change has taken place in post-war capitalist economy, and this has been accompanied by a notable change in capitalist politics and culture as well as lifestyle as parts of the superstructure of capitalist society.

3. A series of major events has occurred in the international communist movement during the post-war years, and many new features of far-reaching and profound significance have appeared in the practice of socialism, giving birth to many phenomena never touched upon or even never anticipated by classical Marxist writers.

4. With the discovery and publication of a huge amount of documents and other data (some of which deserve to be considered first-hand) concerning the history of Marxism and the international communist movement, it has become possible for people to probe anew into those questions which had hitherto baffled them. It is against this highly complex socio-historical background that a host of questions has been raised before Marxism.

We can see that, no matter how erroneous certain viewpoints of the Western "Marxologists" and some "Western Marxists" are according to our stand, the questions they have put forward reflect in a way the rapidly changing world in which we live. To analyse, criticise and answer these questions presupposes studies of the reality of the contemporary world, studies which are realistic instead of *apriorist*, independent instead of parroting the words of others, and comprehensive and systematic instead of abstract.

By and large, the new questions on the international plane fall into the following groups. (Of course, this classification is only relative, for the listed groups crisscross, rather than run parallel to one another, and sometimes questions of one group may give rise to questions of another.)

First, questions concerning the trend of the development of human civilisation.

Since the 1960s, large-scale discussions on the trend of the development of contemporary civilisation have taken place in international academic circles against the background of the scientific-technological revolution. Taking part in these unfolding discussions of far-reaching import are famous social scientists and many top-notch natural scientists. They have advanced what are called the theory of "a society of electronic technology", the theory of "a planned society", the theory of "an informationalised society", the theory of a "post-industrial society", the theory of "the third wave of civilisation", and so on and so forth. Scholars who argue that contemporary civilisation has entered the stage of "an informationalised society" sum up its basic situation as follows:

(1) Human intellectual creativeness replaces simple labour and capital as the source of value.

(2) Changes occur in the activities within industries, giving rise to an information industry whose aim is to create and apply knowledge, science and technology. There is organised circulation of information which is thus made a kind of commodity and whose use becomes a basic factor of human activities.

(3) Education assumes an unprecedented importance,

with most of the spare time of members of society devoted to the acquisition and renewal of knowledge.

The theory of post-industrial society of Daniel Bell holds that, as the most developed country, the United States has entered a post-industrial society which is different from an industrial society in the following ways. In an industrial society, the chief economic problem is that of capital; the "design" of such a society is a "game against fabricated nature" which is centred on man-machine relationships; the chief economic sector is goods producing (manufacturing and processing); and the dominant profession is carried on by semi-skilled workers and engineers. In a post-industrial society, however, the chief problem is the organisation of science; the "design" of such a society is a "game between persons"; the chief economic sector is an "intellectual technology" based on information; society is organised by virtue of scientific-theoretical knowledge so as to control itself and guide the necessary reforms; the dominant profession is carried on by scientists; and the country's scientific capabilities become a decisive factor for its potential and power. Now the United States has gone ahead of the other industrially developed countries which will also enter post-industrial society one by one, irrespective of their different social systems. D. Bell explained that, as a matter of fact, his viewpoints proceed "from Marx", for "Marx defined a mode of production as including both the social relations and the 'forces' (i.e., techniques)." And such "forces" (techniques) are precisely the criterion for judging whether a society is industrial or post-industrial. D. Bell said that "the roots of post-industrial society lie in the inexorable influence of science on productive methods".[6]

I. Prigogine, creator of the "theory of dissipative structure" and one of the most famous of contemporary scientists, thinks that people of the present generation live in the midst of the revolution of information technology, which has touched upon the real core of our culture. A. Toffler said in *The Third Wave* (1980) that, following the waves of the agricultural and the industrial civilisation, the third wave of human civilisation has come. The global problems that have appeared in the fields of ecological environment, population, energy and other resources, economic development, etc., and the disintegration of the original concept of value and the "role system" are the symptoms of the imminent end of industrial civilisation. Resting as it does on the basis of energy, technology and production systems which are vastly different from those characterising the previous two kinds of civilisation, the third wave brings with it a totally new way of social life.

Obviously, what are discussed here are major issues which should necessarily arouse the close attention of Marxists in as much as Marxism takes upon itself the task of revealing the laws of the development of human society. Although the above-stated theories contain erroneous elements and do not have unanimous approval even in the Western world, they also have in themselves certain rational elements. All of them touch on the most fundamental characteristic of modern productive forces, i.e. the decisive role of science and technology, and they use this as a clue in envisaging the trend of development of human civilisation. It must be pointed out in this connection that Marx's foresight was over a century earlier and far more penetrating and brilliant that that of the scholars referred to above. Marx wrote in his *Grundrisse*,

> ". . . To the degree that large industry develops, the creation of real wealth comes to depend less on labour time and on the amount of labour employed than on the power of the agencies set in motion during labour time whose 'powerful effectiveness' is itself in turn out of all proportion to the direct labour time spent on their production, but depends rather on the general state of science and on the progress of technology, or the application of

this science to production."

This indicates,

">". . . to what degree general social knowledge has become a *direct force of production*, and to what degree, hence, the conditions of the process of social life itself have come under the control of the general intellect and been transformed in accordance with it."[7]

The founder of Marxism always differentiated between the various stages of the development of human civilisation in accordance with the characteristics of the specific means of labour and the specific productive forces. "Social relations are closely bound up with productive forces. In acquiring new productive forces men change their mode of production; and in changing their mode of production, in changing the way of earning their living, they change all their social relations."[8] Since they regard science and technology as the most important productive force in the modern era, and since they have witnessed the powerful role of science and technology as a productive force in the development of contemporary civilisation, contemporary Marxists cannot evade making a theoretically profound analysis of the following questions:

Is it true that modern science and technology have ushered human civilisation into a new stage of development? If not, why? If yes, what then are the overall characteristics of this higher stage of human civilisation? What are the differences between this and the previous stage? What new social structures and relations has the new civilisation brought in its wake?

Is the new civilisation a common stage of social development into which all nations and countries must necessarily enter? Or is it a form of development peculiar to the capitalist countries? If it is the first, what specific forms of expression will it assume in countries of different social systems? In particular, what attitude should China — a country with relatively backward science and technology — take to this new wave of civilisation? If the new civilisation in question is a form of development peculiar to the capitalist countries, will this be a challenge to the validity of a series of major Marxist theories of capitalism (e.g., the labour theory of value in the context of scientific and technological advance, the effect of the scientific-technological revolution on the class structure in capitalist society, etc.)?

Second, questions occasioned by the new characteristics of contemporary capitalist development.

Capitalism experienced a rather long period of relative prosperity following the close of World War II. Although the present-day capitalist world generally suffers from sluggishness or stagnation and from serious crises (economic, political, social, cultural, etc.), it is obviously hard to say with certainty that the total collapse of capitalism is already in sight. Hence the renewal of the discussion on the "resilience of capitalism". Some theorists of Eurocommunism assert that, after each relatively big crisis, capitalism can restabilise itself, and that Marx did not foresee this at all. H. Marcuse holds that this is something even Lenin failed to foresee.[9] If it is true that capitalism can, to a certain extent, adapt itself to the impact of the scientific-technological revolution (productive forces of a new type), of the conflict between labour and capital, of the production crisis, etc., we would like to ask; to what specific extent can capitalism adapt itself to such impacts? What is its inner mechanism in this connection?

People can see that the inner mechanism of capitalism's adaptability to these circumstances includes the evolution of ownership towards nationalisation, the strengthening of the regulatory role of the state, the improvement of measures for social welfare, and the changes in social structures and class relations. These can be briefly described as follows:

The capitalist countries have tried to increase the proportion of capitalist state ownership by nationalising private corporations, or establishing mixed corporations under state-private ownership, or directly establishing new state-run enterprises. Accordingly, direct economic interference and regulation by the capitalist state have been greatly enhanced. This means regulating social production through the credit system and tax policy; ensuring a high depreciation rate for enterprises through legal channels so as to greatly induce investment in production techniques; the state actively participating in the distribution and redistribution of national income; the various capitalist countries taking unified actions for monopolistic regulation of an international character; and so on. What is most outstanding is long-term planning by the capitalist state.

State ownership does not necessarily mean socialism.[10] The fact is that ownership by the capitalist state has only partially replaced private capital and private ownership in the capitalist countries, and capitalism has not been uprooted. But can we take the spread of such state ownership and the continued increase of the state's regulatory role in the economic process to mean that a partial qualitative change has occurred in the development of capitalism, that is to say, there is now a new stage of capitalism's development? It is not totally without reason that some Yugoslav scholars use the term "state capitalism" in describing the above characteristics of contemporary capitalism and call its state system "totalitarianism".[11] Marx and Engels regarded as one of capitalism's basic contradictions that between organised production within specific capitalist enterprises and the anarchy in production of capitalist society as a whole. What change will take place in this basic contradiction, with the enhancing of the state regulatory role of the contemporary capitalist state and, consequently, with the addition of a new mechanism to the laws of the market and value? Basing themselves on the above-mentioned phenomena, some "Western Marxists" and Communist theorists in the developed capitalist countries[12] have tried to substantiate the following thesis. It is that in the development of contemporary capitalism, the state plays the role of an effective stabiliser for capitalist economy, and this makes outmoded the division of society into the "economic base" and the "superstructure", for politics ceases to be part of the superstructure and the activities of the government and political struggles are now incorporated into the functions of the economic base. The contemporary capitalist state plays the role of protecting the organism of society and ensuring the entire process of expanded reproduction. Such a state is at once a capitalist state and one independent of the various strata of the capitalist class. The emergence of such a kind of modern state makes it necessary to reappraise Lenin's thesis of the state being purely an instrument for exploiting the oppressed classes. And in the developed capitalist countries it is no longer necessary for the socialist revolution to smash the existing state machine; what needs to be done is merely to make the state "undergo transformation and conversion", establish the orthodoxy of the democratic state on a new basis, enable the state to really reflect the popular will and successfully administer the big enterprises, and eventually place it under supervision by the people.

Evidently, it is fallacious to blur the demarcation line between the economic base and the superstructure, for this can only deprive historical materialism of its scientific character in this analysis of the phenomena of social life. It is also fallacious to deny wholesale the relevant revolutionary thesis of Lenin's, for this can only make the proletariat in many countries lose sight of the prospects of the revolution. Nevertheless, confronted as we are with the new characteristics of the functions of the contemporary capitalist state, we should undoubtedly pay adequate attention to the question of how the Communist Parties in different countries ought to explore, in the light of the actual realities in their own countries, the specific roads of the socialist revolution there.

In close connection with the above questions, we have the question of the possibility and the specific roads of the proletarian revolution in contemporary capitalist countries with their material affluence. Since the end of World War II, all major capitalist countries have taken varied and energetic measures for social welfare so as to alleviate the labour-capital contradictions. These include the well-known measures for ensuring high wages and salaries, high commodity prices and a high level of consumption; for ensuring social welfare services including labour protection and relief to the unemployed; and for ensuring lifelong employment, and even the job inheritance system as practised in some Japanese enterprises. Where the welfare policy is unable to fully play its role due to mounting difficulties, the capitalist enterprises are paying more and more attention to the question of increasing the workers' role in enterprise activities by way of drawing them onto the boards of directors and thus allowing them to take part in management.

On this basis, the Frankfurt school has advanced the theory of "the affluent society", which maintains that contemporary capitalist society has essentially changed the status of the proletariat; that the technological conditions of a highly industrialised society have created affluence which can satisfy people's needs, so much so that the causes of discontent and protest are got rid of there; that the proletariat's attitude of "absolute negation" to the existing system has changed to one of affirming and supporting it; and that the cause of revolution will cease to be economic exploitation, for this will be replaced by repression of some human instincts.[13] Using the Freudian theory to interpret basic social problems is naturally very absurd. Proceeding from the standpoint of historical materialism that man's social being determines his social consciousness, however, we cannot ignore the following question: whence the revolutionary consciousness of the proletariat living under the material conditions in the developed capitalist countries? Or, how can the proletariat there come to realise the necessity of revolution? Should we not cast aside the vulgar and simplified view which looks at things merely from the angle of economic life, and return to Marx's theory of estrangement criticising the sum total of capitalism and regard the crisis of contemporary capitalism as steadily deepening and shifting from the sphere of material life to the political, social, spiritual and cultural spheres? In this context, our criticism of the harm contemporary capitalism does mankind should not be a mere repetition of the portrayal of the appalling material privations of the 18th and 19th centuries, but should go deep into the debasement of the value of man by the capitalist mode of production and way of life, and into their destruction of the basic relationship between man and nature (e.g., the ecological crisis). It may be assumed that the rise of revolution under contemporary capitalist conditions will be due to the yearning not for mere economic emancipation but for the perfection of all the social relations between man, the enrichment of men's spiritual life and the establishment of a harmonious relationship between men and nature — "the emergence of nature for man"[14] — all on the premise of man's economic emancipation. To put it in a nutshell, it will be due to the yearning for the elimination of all forms of estrangement (economic, political, social, cultural and psychological) and for the perfection of human existence.

The question of class structure in the contemporary developed capitalist countries has also to be considered. Along with the increasing preponderance of science and technology in contemporary capitalist production, the middle class consisting of the managerial, scientific and technological personnel is increasing in number and playing a more and more important role in society. R. Dahrendorf said that "the Marxian notion of a society split into two antagonistic classes growing out of the property structure of the economy is no longer a correct description of European reality."[15] And according to A. Giddens, the growth of a large white-collar middle class, located predominantly within the service sector of the economy, constitutes "a fundamental stumbling block to Marxist theory".[16] In refuting the views of bourgeois scholars, some "Western Marxists" try to substantiate that the new middle class is an unstable economic composite made up of people whose status is between the proletariat and the bourgeoisie; and that the union of these people depends on their ideological and political functions in the socio-economic system. Some other "Western Marxists" hold that the concept of "wage class" can be used in this very connection, a concept which can replace that of "working class" in the traditional sense Marx had in mind.

Here we are discussing not merely concepts but the question of the validity of Marx's theory on the proletarian revolution. If the proletariat ceased to be the basic labouring class in contemporary capitalist society, who would be the revolutionary force for overthrowing capitalism? Since, in some oriental countries, where the working class used to be extremely small in number and relatively weak in strength, the alliance of the proletariat with the peasantry, the petty bourgeoisie and even the national bourgeoisie led to the victory of the revolution, can we assume that the revolutionary force in the developed capitalist countries would be the alliance of the proletariat with the overwhelming majority of the middle class? In point of fact, Eurocommunism has already put forward views like this. We cannot answer the above questions simply by citing some relevant passages from classical Marxist writings, for they have come to be studied independently by applying the basic methodology of Marxism.

Third, there are questions that have newly cropped up in the international communist movement.

Stalin's death in 1953 and the dissolution in 1956 of the Information Bureau of the Communist and Workers' Parties heralded the end of a period in the history of the international communist movement, a period which was marked by the domination of "one centre, one road and one model". Marxists of the various countries, proceeding from the concrete realities in their own lands, began to explore the specific roads along which their respective countries could advance to socialism-communism, thus bringing about a new situation in the contemporary international communist movement where diversity has replaced stereotype. Even today some people still frown upon this situation and attempt to resort to the role of the baton once again. For our part, however, we are truly happy to see this trend towards varied development, a trend which is fully in accord with historical dialectics. Diversified practice will undoubtedly verify from many angles the general principles of Marxism and thus immensely enrich the theory of scientific communism.

Following World War II, there has occurred a series of major historical events, such as the expulsion of Yugoslavia from the Information Bureau of the Communist and Workers' Parties, the criticism of Stalin by the Twentieth Congress of the CPSU, the Polish and Hungarian incidents of 1956, the Sino-Soviet polemics, China's "cultural revolution", the "Prague Spring" and its suppression, the Soviet invasion of Afghanistan, the Vietnamese invasion of Kampuchea and the victory and defeat of the Kampuchean Communist Party, the military control of Poland, the series of conflicts between the Albanian Party of Labour and the Communist and Workers' Parties of other countries, the nationalist movement within the Soviet "community of nations", and the rise and evolution of Eurocommunism. All these events have put a series of sharp questions before Marxism, which we should never evade, for otherwise Marxism and socialism will suffer in prestige. We should collect first-hand data and study the questions carefully and on the basis of facts so that we can arrive at Marxist conclusions instead of leaving a blank in the theory of Marxism as far as this eventful period is concerned.

The discovery and publication of an enormous body of literature and other data concerning the history of the international communist movement — e.g. the publication of the deleted parts of the text of the previous editions of Lenin's *Works*; of the daily records written by Lenin's secretary during his illness; of Lenin's will; of the memoirs of some famous persons and their letters to family members; of the original data regarding some major events; and of many unofficial histories whose authenticity we should naturally ascertain — have made it possible to reassess many important events and personalities in the history of the international communist movement. This means reassessment of, for instance, "War Communism", the "New Economic Policy", Stalin's "road to industrialisation" and his "revolution from top to bottom", the truth of the magnification of the scope of the Soviet struggle against the counter-revolutionaries, the historical role of the Third International, the relationship between Trotsky and the Fourth International, and the theories of Rosa Luxemburg,

Nikolai Bukharin and Antonio Gramsci. The publication of the works Lenin wrote shortly before his death and the related background material has all the more aroused the interest of people in his thinking in the evening of his life. During his later years Lenin found that, despite the great successes of the cause initiated by the October Revolution, it suffered from quite a few defects and inadequacies, and that is why he raised the questions of democratising the organs of the proletarian dictatorship and the Soviets, of opposing bureaucratism and over-concentration of powers, and of giving full play to the role of co-operatives. Stalin deviated from Lenin's thinking on these questions, and this led to serious tragedy for the Soviet Party and state as well as for Stalin himself. Studies of what has been described above will not only help restore the true features of history but also have a direct bearing on the contemporary development of Marxism.

To advance Marxism we should give adequate attention to the comparative studies of the socialist system. This means studying the different roads taken by different countries in socialist construction under relatively different historical conditions, and exploring and summarising the relevant laws on the basis of their specific experiences and lessons. Marx, Engels and Lenin spent the greater part of their energies in seeking the road of revolution for overthrowing capitalism. Although they all scientifically foresaw quite a lot about construction in the economic and political fields following the revolutionary victory, they did not formulate for us — and could not possibly have done so — any systematic and specific theories in this respect due to lack of practical experience or time. For their part, Stalin and Mao Zedong performed outstanding deeds in guiding the practice of socialism. Nonetheless, both of them made gross miscalculations which find expression in their respective theories. In the international context, it can be said, therefore, that there are many gaps to be filled in the Marxist theories concerning socialist construction. (Here "construction" is taken in its broad sense, i.e., construction in the economic, political, social, cultural and other spheres.)

The comparative studies of the socialist system involve several groups of questions. The first group of questions includes those arising out of socialism changing from theory into reality, questions which are of universal significance for all socialist countries. For instance, compared with the period of revolutionary wars, what unmistakable changes has the Communist Party undergone as a ruling party, and what other changes may it possibly undergo in the future? We should also study the subsequent questions: What are the laws of building such a ruling party? That is to say, for instance, what are the laws of its organisational and ideological construction and of the democratic life within its own ranks? And what should be its organisational and ideological principles? What are the special difficulties in the succession of the older people in the Party's leadership by the younger (i.e., difficulties in the training of successors)? And how can these difficulties be overcome? Other major questions concern the relationship between the Party and society, that is, the question of the respective powers and responsibilities of the ruling party and the state organs; the question of leaders-party-class-masses under conditions where the Communist Party has become the ruling party; the question of the relationship between the activities of the ruling party and the legal system of the country; and the questions of the relationship between the ruling party on the one hand and the trade union, the women's federation, the youth league and other mass organisations on the other. Finally, there are the series of questions which the socialist state must solve, e.g. the question of contradictions among the people and class struggle in socialist society, the question of building a high level of socialist democracy, the question of democratic centralism, and the question of the relations among the various nationalities in the country.

The second group of questions to be studied are those arising out of socialism becoming a reality first in a single country and then also in other countries. In a certain period of time, the socialist state which is born earlier than others will unavoidably be looked upon by the latter as their model. After a period of specific practice, however, these latter countries will unavoidably meet with many-sided disharmonies resulting from mechanical copying of the experiences of the first socialist state. Even this first socialist state itself may, in due course, find that the model it has designed for its own building of socialism is incapable of suiting the objective reality in many respects. Hence the question whether there should be changes in the model itself and whether the other countries should avoid mechanically copying the foreign model. Yugoslavia's creation of the socialist self-management system and its evolution, and the reforms in economic and political systems carried out on different scales by countries of the Soviet camp since the 1960s — all these are precisely a reflection of this point. We should make emphatical studies of the experiences — both positive and negative — in such experiments and reforms of different types and compare the different social and economic results of the different reform programmes and concrete measures. (These results include the degree of social stability, the degree of democratisation, the extent to which the social structures are suited to objective reality, economic effectiveness, the level of labour productivity, and the level of scientific and technological development).

Also among the questions arising out of socialism changing from reality in a single country to reality in some other countries are the following: the principles guiding the mutual relations of the Communist Parties as ruling parties; the relationship between proletarian internationalism of the socialist countries on the one hand and national independence and national interests on the other; the appraisal by one Communist Party of the ideologies of its counterparts in other countries; the economic co-operation and the so-called "international division of labour" among the various socialist countries; and the conflicts and contradictions among the socialist countries.

The third group of questions requiring comparative study concerns the peculiar laws of socialist construction in underdeveloped countries. Almost all those countries which underwent revolution resulting in the birth of a new regime after World War II are underdeveloped ones. This seems to have forecast a historical trend having the character of a law. Objective revolutionary reality has brought many complex factors into the process of historical development, factors which the classical theses of Marxism did not foresee, at least not fully. The revolution in underdeveloped countries has greatly enriched and developed Marxism. How these countries should undertake socialist construction in a scientific manner following the trimph of the revolution — this has posed to Marxism more questions which are even more complex. For, compared with the process of transition of the developed capitalist countries to socialism as envisaged by Marx and Engels, the transition process of the underdeveloped countries has far richer characteristics. Prior to the revolution, a fair proportion of the socio-economic formation of these latter countries had not yet advanced to the stage of capitalism, retaining certain feudal and semi-colonial and semi-feudal elements or even certain elements of serfdom and the clan system. The establishment of socialist state power has enabled them to skip over the stage of capitalism. What, under socio-historical conditions where they do not have the material prerequisite of a developed commodity economy and where the general educational level of their people is not high and there is a general lack of tradition of democratic life, — what, under these conditions, are their experiences and lessons in developing socialist commodity economy, in handling the contradiction between strengthening their weak basis of production and technology and raising the low living standard of their people, in assessing the role of science, education, culture and the intellectuals in socialist contruction, in eradicating the corrosive influence of the pre-capitalist social relations, psychology and ideology over the new society, etc.? In view of the fact that most of these countries had the bitter experience of imperialist aggression, we should study how they are to uproot the imperialist influence and handle the relationship between receiving the impetus of the advanced scientific, cultural and economic achievements of foreign countries on the one hand, and preserving their own national dignity and independence on the other.

Fourth, there are questions concerning the basic theories of Marxism itself, which have come to the fore following the publication of a large amount of Marx's manuscripts, especially those written in his early years.

The link between Marx as a young man and Marx in his old age occasions different responses. Some scholars totally negate the works Marx wrote when he was young, whereas most others do their utmost to praise such works at the expense of Marx's mature theories. It is clear that both approaches to Marxism are unscientific and are designed to cast an image of Marx according the respective political and ideological requirements of the people concerned. We should study the development of Marx's thinking as an organic and integrated process and give truth-seeking answers to the difficult questions concerning it, such as the relationship between the theory of estrangement and historical materialism, between the concepts of species and the theory of class struggle, between freedom and determinism, between philosophy and political economy, etc. We must find out what are the factors in the thinking of the young Marx which he really abandoned afterwards? And what are the factors which disappeared later only in form but were, in essence, incorporated into the inner depths of his mature theories? What are the theses which were later presented in a different way or were, for the time being, not presented altogether out of tactical considerations (e.g., for better publicity among the toiling masses who were yet philosophically immature, and for greater flexibility and initiative in polemics with exponents of different schools of thought)?

There is also the relationship between Marxism and humanism to consider. For a long period, this question remained a forbidden area of study in China. Today, however, fewer and fewer people still refuse to admit that there is humanism in Marxism. Even L. Althusser, who declared that Marxism was "anti-humanism", can now say so only in the sense of methodology, i.e., of structuralist methodology which sets science against value. Nevertheless, many questions in this respect call for in-depth studies. If humanism is contained in Marxism, what position does it occupy there? Does it constitute one aspect (an element or a thesis) of Marxism? Or is it embodied as a general spirit in the overall programme for social reform envisaged by Marxism? What is the relationship between Marxist humanism on the one hand and humanism of the previous historical periods and contemporary bourgeois humanism on the other? What are the essential features of Marxist humanism, which fundamentally set it apart from all the other forms of humanism? What is the practical significance of Marxist humanism for contemporary capitalism and contemporary socialism?

Also of interest is the relationship between science and ideology in Marxism. Since Marx's *Economic-Philosophical Manuscripts of 1844* possess a stronger ethical colour than his later writings, some Western scholars seem to have discovered here another Marx. In a book review appearing in the *New York Times*, S. Hook wrote that, when Marx descended to the world a second time, he did not do so as the author of *Capital* or a busy economist, nor as a revolutionary *sans culotte* or the author of the inspiring *Communist Manifesto*. He reappeared in the robe of a philosopher or moralist, Hook added. Another scholar said that the premise of Marx's theories was not, as explained by Marxism, scientific principles, but, rather, *a priori* philosophical principles with the character of a belief.

Thus, the question of the relationship between science and ideology in Marxism has once again been raised in a sharp manner. In fact, this question can be traced back to the period of the Second International. Kautsky and company declared that Marxism was an empirical science, and that it could not be called philosophy because the materialist viewpoint meant an empirical viewpoint and nothing else. This argument led to an erroneous viewpoint in history, that Marxism supposedly never had a philosophy of its own, let alone its own concept of value. So the neo-Kantians tried to "supplement" Marxism with the ethical theory in Kantian philosophy, advancing "ethical socialism" as a counterpoint to Kautsky's vulgar viewpoint. In the contemporary era this question also appears in other forms, for instance: "Is Marxism a science, or a concept of value?" The heart of the controversy lies in the following: is Marx's idea about communism based on the objective trend of the development of society itself? Or does it rely merely on some beautiful ideal about the future of mankind?

We must pay close attention to the above questions,

for they are also practical questions often met in our country. It is extremely wrong to boil down scientific socialism merely to a kind of belief about the future — as some Western scholars have done — because this implies an attempt to reduce Marxism to a kind of religious belief. On the other hand, it is likewise wrong to completely deny that Marxism has its own concept of value. Are we not criticising the theory in China that "communisum is but a dim illusion" and advocating a firm communist ideal and conviction? We should persist in the unity of science and value in Marxism. In *Capital*, Marx affirmed that "the evolution of the economic formation of society is viewed as a process of natural history",[17] and held that the objective laws of historical development should be revealed in the same way as the physical phenomena are revealed with the aid of physics and as the life phenomena are revealed with the aid of biology. (This is what is meant by Marxism as a science.) At the same time, Marx firmly believed that, with the attainment of communism, men will be able to live "under conditions most favourable to, and worthy of, their human nature".[18] (This is what is meant by Marxism as a concept of value.)

Finally, there is the link between Marx on the one hand and Engels and Lenin on the other. Most Western scholars have striven to find some sort of "contradiction" between Marx and the other two. For instance, they have tried to substantiate that Marx's philosophical outlook is "humanism" whereas Engels' is "positivism-scientism"; that Marx defined dialectics as the contradictory structure of human practice whereas Engels indiscriminately applied dialectics to the natural world;[19] that Marx revealed that man's relationship with the object meant *praxis* whereas Engels and Lenin mechanically understood it as "reflection";[20] that Marx and Engels regarded the high-level development of capitalism and the numerical superiority of the proletariat as an indispensable precondition for the socialist revolution wereas Lenin neglected them and merely believed in a small number of the Blanqui-type revolutionaries inciting the people to make revolution; that "for Marx the concept of dictatorship is primarily social and economic ... For Lenin 'dictatorship' is primarily a political concept"[21]; and that Marx resorted to the self-emancipation of the proletariat whereas Lenin stressed the proletariat's emancipation by its vanguard. There are many more similar arguments. All are utterly serious challenges, some of which contain obvious misrepresentation and ill will. As negative examples, they compel us to conduct conscientious studies of the entire development of Marxism and Leninism and to give it a well-founded and logical interpretation. Failing to do so will mean that we are incapable both of answering the challenges of our opponents and of convincing people of good will who have doubts and misgivings.

III. To develop Marxism within overall reform, and build socialism with Chinese characteristics

It is self-evident that, in studying Marxism under contemporary conditions, the Chinese Marxists should, first and foremost, use the "arrow" of Marxism to shoot at the "target" of China's revolution and construction. China is a big country; the Chinese Communist Party is a big political party; the Chinese revolution followed a long, tortuous path; and in its practice of socialism China has gained a considerable body of valuable experiences and profound lessons. With such a rich and vivid reality as the object of their studies and summarising the related experiences and lessons in real earnest, the Chinese theoretical workers can certainly make unique contributions to the development of Marxism in the world as a whole.

Many comrades have realised that China's theoretical

work lags, in a fairly large measure, behind the vigorous development of practical life. Since the Third Plenary Session of its Eleventh Central Committee, the Chinese Communist Party has boldly carried out a series of momentous reforms and other creative undertakings. Many of the new things that have come to the fore in real life, and many new experiences that have been accumulated, baffle people's imagination. Most outstanding among the reforms is the adoption of the output-related responsibility system in agricultural production. There are no ready-made formulas in classical Marxist writings for this system to go by; it has no position in the traditional norms (just the contrary, it is considered as one that runs against taboos); and there are no counterparts in the various existing models abroad. Such a responsibility system is a unique creation beyond all conventions. By comparison, certain aspects of our theoretical work have fallen behind, for they still revolve around some "antiques", concerning themselves, as before, with some abstract conclusions which are divorced from real life and thus appear shrivelled and pallid. This provides a sanctuary and hotbed for the "Left" ideology and offers an ideological ground on the basis of which exponents of such ideology can censure the current reforms. If this state of affairs is allowed to continue, it will become an obstacle to the cause of reform launched under the guidance of the Party since the Third Plenary Session of its Eleventh Central Committee. Consequently, the Chinese theoretical workers face the most urgent, most important and most sacred task of studying how to carry out overall reforms and chart China's own path of building socialism with Chinese characteristics. This has much to do with the future of China, the future of China's theoretical work and the prospects for the development of Marxism in this country.

Lenin said with profound meaning, "All nations will

arrive at socialism — this is inevitable, but all will do so in not exactly the same way, each will contribute something of its own to some form of democracy, to some variety of the dictatorship of the proletariat, to the varying rate of socialist transformations in the different aspects of social life."[22] Our Party has defined Mao Zedong Thought as the integration of the universal truth of Marxism with the concrete practice of the Chinese revolution. And Comrade Deng Xiaoping, Vice-Chairman of the Chinese Communist Party's Central Committee, has put forth the guiding principle of "building socialism with Chinese characteristics", which represents a creative development of Mao Zedong Thought.

"Building socialism with Chinese characteristics" is a programmatic thesis that has two points as its main content: One is "socialism", and the other "Chinese characteristics". To satisfy the requirements of these two aspects and fulfil our great programme, it is first of all necessary for us to study socialism by tracing back to its origin and distinguishing socialism from the specific model which was held up as an immutable formula in the past decades. We should find out what theses the founders of scientific socialism advanced with regard to socialist-communist society. Which of these are of univeral significance, i.e. what are the fundamental aspects that must necessarily be observed by all nations and countries in building socialism? And which are of restricted significance, i.e., what are the aspects that were expounded in classical Marxist writings under the influence of specific historical and regional conditions? What, in Lenin's momentous development of scientific socialism, are the principles which are universally applicable? And what are the particular conclusions which, being applicable only to the specific socio-historical conditions in Russia, should not be mechanically copied everywhere? Which of Stalin's and

Mao Zedong's expositions on socialism are really a development of Marxism-Leninism? And which must necessarily be discarded? Moreover, we should study the expositions of socialism made, in the various stages of the development of Marxism, by many prominent figures worthy of being called leaders and thinkers, and see which really represent deep insight and which were only of transitory significance? If we fail to study socialism by getting to its very root, we will find it very difficult to grasp its essence and refrain from regarding this or that model appearing in the practice of socialism as one of its universal principles.

We are also required to make unprecedented and comprehensive studies of our own country. It goes without saying that what imparts Chinese characteristics to the universal system of socialism (i.e., socialism which will be practised by all nations in the future) is China's specific conditions — its history, culture, people, their habits and psychology as well as way of life, the country's current economic and political situations, its physical features, ecological environment, etc. Only penetrating studies of these conditions can enable us to find the best way of combining the basic system of socialism (the general features and principles) with China's specific conditions (the particular features and given reality). In the past we made quite a number of detours and, in some respects, acted in a regretable manner because, apart from our failure to have a really accurate grasp of socialism, we did not conscientiously study these conditions and even failed to realise the necessity of doing so. This being so, naturally we could not carry out the optimum combinations of the two aspects mentioned above. What should be the distinguishing features of the economic structure, the political structure, the family structure, the social relations, the cultural structure, the psychological structure, and the ideological structure under socialism with Chinese characteristics? We can gradually understand all these only through prolonged exploration and experiments in the creative spirit of Marxism and by the various advanced methods of contemporary natural and social sciences.

Building socialism with Chinese characteristics is our general objective while overall reform is the only effective way of achieving it. As far as the building of socialism by different countries is concerned, there should be no *standardised* model; as far as the building of socialism in an individual country is concerned, there should be no *immutable* model. To accomplish the four modernisations of China (modernisation of its industry, agriculture, national defence, and science and technology), it is imperative to introduce a series of reforms which should run through the entire process. This should become an exceedingly important area for our Party in guiding the progress of socialist modernisation. We should expound the Marxist outlook of reform in accordance with the basic principles of historical materialism. As socialist society is a new, steadily developing formation, there is, in relation to the ever-growing social productive forces, a process of continuously perfecting the socialist production relations and the superstructure in order to suit, protect and uninterruptedly promote the growth of the productive forces. *The necessity for reform is, therefore, determined by the very character of socialism.* More than once the founder of Marxism said that the change of the process of social advance from a spontaneous process to a consciously guided process is one of the basic indicators of mankind's transition from the realm of necessity to the realm of freedom. If it can be said that, under private ownership, social development is realised through confrontation and conflicts, socialism is realised through planned reforms which are guided by scientific theories. This is exactly where the characteristics and advantages of socialism's planned development lie. All revolutionaries should see that their thinking advances along with the advance of history. They should readily absorb whatever new ideas, results of creative efforts and new experiences conform to the interests of the people and the requirements of the era. They should be bold enough to give up whatever conventions, regulations and old work styles that do not suit the new historical task and the requirements of revolutionary practice. We should enable all Party comrades, and cadres at all levels in particular, to understand that reform means a consistent principle of the dynamic and creative cause of socialism.

In his report "On Questions of China's Four Modernisations and Reform", Comrade Hu Yaobang, Chairman of the Central Committee of the Chinese Communist Party, made clear that our general principle should be for us to proceed from actual reality and carry out the reform comprehensively and systematically, and determinedly and methodically. This calls for systematic studies of the reform theories, comprehensively comparing and studying the advantages and disadvantages of the various reforms made in foreign countries, and foreseeing the problems that may crop up in the process of the reform in China so that a scientific programme and the related measures can be worked out for it. We should, in this connection, be especially good at summarising the experiences gained in the current reforms and replace the old theories and principles that practice has proved utterly unworkable with new ones that have been verified as correct in real life. Many comrades have long since realised that the chief inadequacy in our economic system is that it lacks vitality, that is to say, our enterprises do not have proper initiative and proper flexibility in work and that their workers and staff members lack due enthusiasm and a sense of responsibility. We may go a step further and ask with good reason: with public ownership of the means of production established in our socialist society and with the possibilities of capitalist society's contradiction between the social character of production and the private ownership of the means of production eliminated, why cannot our economic systems fully develop their vitality? The reform of the system of China's agricultural production is highly evocative, for within a few years of its inception, springtime has come to our agriculture which is thus experiencing a new lease of life. So the lack of vitality in our economic systems cannot be attributed to the socialist system itself. Whoever doubts this point will commit grave mistakes. The heart of the matter lies in the economic structure and backward forms of management which cannot suit the development of the productive forces. Experiences — both positive and negative — over the past decades tell us that the form of ownership must be suited to the character and level of the productive forces. We should not put everything under state ownership or state operation. Under the conditions prevailing in China, we should carry out reform in the structure of ownership and permit the coexistence of varied economic forms on the premise that the leading position of the state economy is ensured. Furthermore, an advanced structure of ownership has to be accompanied by advanced forms of management. Otherwise, we shall be unable to give full play to the superiority of the socialist production relations. Consequently, we should think more deeply and see whether, in China's political, ideological, cultural and other parts of the superstructure, there are any systems, rules, regulations and customary ways of doing things which have been influenced by foreign models and which, though we ourselves regard them as being in conformity with the socialist standards, in fact hamstring the full display of the superiority of socialism and restrict the full development of the creativeness of the people in different fields of endeavour. As set forth by the Twelfth National Congress of the Chinese Communist Party held in September 1982, we should strive for a high level of democracy in the political sphere, a high level of material civilisation in the sphere of material life, and a high level of socialist spiritual civilisation in the sphere of spiritual life. Without boldly breaking through the outmoded and ossified conventions and regulations that clash with the interests of the people, it will be hard to fulfil the magnificent goals described above. What reforms should be initiated in the superstructure of Chinese society so that we can sweep away the obstacles to the development of the vitality of our system and so that all members of our socialist society can display their vigourous and mounting enthusiasm, creativeness and initiative in the vast fields of the production of both material and spiritual values, and in the political life of the country and the community life at the grass roots? In a word, the many reforms we should carry out are related to the questions put before Chinese Marxists by the contemporary world and by China itself. We should broaden our vision and boldly explore the various possibilities. To build socialism with Chinese characteristics is a great undertaking never attempted by our forefathers. Many aspects of the different structures formed in the past three decades and more do not accord with the requirements of this general objective of ours, so they must be reformed. Without reform, it will be out of the question to build socialism with Chinese characteristics and develop Marxism under the specific conditions in China.

*   *   *

In a speech that initiated a new pattern of development for 20th-century mathematics, David Hilbert, one of the greatest mathematicians of the present century, called *"questions" the inherent motive force of the development of science*. It is beyond doubt that only those theories which are closely combined with human practice can meet one new question after another. The fact that a theory is not challenged by objective reality means that it has already been spurned by real life, that it has already died out. That in the contemporary era a host of questions has posed a challenge to Marxism does not mean that Marxism is now "in crisis" or "on the verge of bankruptcy". On the contrary, it attests to the bright future that lies in store for Marxism, which will undoubtedly acquire unlimited motive force for advance in the effort to seek answers to those questions. With his great genius and wisdom, tenacious will, devoted spirit in seeking truth, and lofty and serious sense of responsibility to history, Marx made profound and systematic studies of the weightiest, most pressing and most baffling questions raised by world history when it had advanced to the mid-19th century. Based on a full understanding and critical assimilation of all the valuable achievements in human thought, his studies gave convincing answers to these questions, and forcefully proved that his theories are the direct and worthy continuation of the most valuable theories representative of the thinking of mankind in the previous epochs. Marx thus won for himself an unfading prestige in the history of human thought, and earned wholehearted admiration and lasting commemoration by progressive people of all countries in different epochs. Provided that with the same spirit, will and sense of responsibility as those of Marx, we make a fair appraisal and critical use of all the major results mankind has obtained in natural and social sciences during the century after Marx, and carry out profound and systematic studies of, and give convincing answers to, the weightiest, most pressing and most baffling questions raised by world history (including the history of China itself) when it has advanced to the closing years of the 20th century — provided that we can do all this, we shall be able to prove the following with the *contemporary* achievements of Marxism: Marxism has absolutely nothing resembling sectarianism, and it is absolutely not a conservative and hardened theory *deviating from* the broad path of the development of world civilisation but a theory which is rooted in the ever-developing practice of mankind and has a great, inexhaustible vitality. We shall, then, be worthy of the glorious title of successor to the cause of Marx, and shall not feel ashamed before the portrait of this great revolutionary teacher.

Footnotes

1. Engels' "Preface to the German Edition of 1890" in Marx and Engels, *The Communist Manifesto*, Foreign Languages Press, Beijing, 1965, p.22.
2. See "Theme for the 1982 Round Table in Cavtat, Yugoslavia (International Forum "Socialism in the World").
3. L. Althusser, "The Crisis of Marxism", *Marxism Today*, July 1978.
4. "Speech at the Chinese Communist Party's National Conference on Propaganda Work", *Selected Works of Mao Zedong*, Foreign Languages Press, Beijing, 1977, Vol. V, p.434.
5. Daniel Bell, *The Social Sciences Since the Second World War*.
6. Daniel Bell, *The Coming of Post-Industrial Society*, Basic Books Inc., Publishers, New York, 1973, p.378.
7. Marx, *Grundrisse (Foundations of the Critique of Political Economy Rough Draft)*, Penguin Books Ltd., Harmondsworth, 1974, pp.704-6.
8. Marx, *The Poverty of Philosophy*, Foreign Languages Press, Beijing, 1978, p.103.
9. See H. Marcuse, *Soviet Marxism*, New York, 1961, p.30.
10. See Engels, *Anti-Dühring*, FLP, Beijing, 1976, p. 359.
11. See Predrag Vranicki, *Marksizam i Socijalizam*, Zagreb, 1979, chapter 3, section 1.
12. See reports in *Asahi Journal* of Japan, August 3rd, 1979, and in *Akahata* of July 17-19, 1979, on an international theoretical forum sponsored by the Japanese Communist Party.
13. See David McLellan, *Marxism After Marx*, chapter 19.
14. From Marx's *Economic-Philosophical Manuscripts of 1844*.
15. R. Dahrendorf, *Recent Changes in the Class Structure of European Societies*, Daedalus, 1964, pp.127-28.
16. A. Giddens, *The Class Structure of the Advanced Societies*, Barnes & Noble, New York, 1973, pp.101, 188.

17. Marx, *Capital*, Progress Publishers, Moscow, 1965, Vol. I, p.10.
18. *Ibid.*, Foreign Languages Publishing House, Moscow, 1959, Vol. III, p.800.
19. See R. Aronson, *The Individualist Social Theory of Jean-Paul Sartre* (1977).
20. See L. Kolakowski, *Main Currents of Marxism*, (1978), Vol. I, chapter 16 and Vol. II, chapter 17.
21. S. Hook, *Revolution, Reform and Social Justice*, New York University Press, 1975, p. 88.
22. Lenin, *Collected Works*, Progress Publishers, Moscow, 1964, Vol. 23, p.69.

II

The Asiatic Mode of Production in History as Viewed by Political Economy in Its Broad Sense

Wu Dakun

I. The position of the theory of the Asiatic mode of production in Marxist political economy in its broad sense

Political economy can be understood in two senses: one is political economy in a narrow sense, i.e., that which is devoted to the study of the capitalist mode of production; the other is political economy in a broad sense, i.e., political economy "as the science of the conditions and forms under which the various human societies have produced and exchanged and have always correspondingly distributed their products".[1] Founded by Marx, this political economy in a broad sense is for the overall critique of bourgeois economics. For "it was not enough to be acquainted with the capitalist form of production, exchange and distribution. The forms preceding it or still existing alongside it in less developed countries had also to be examined and compared, at least in their main features."[2] This is the reason why, along with his examination of the capitalist mode of production, Marx carefully studied the various pre-capitalist ones. The results of his studies of these pre-capitalist modes of production were incorporated into the related chapters of *Capital*, Marx's most important work, and also in the section "Pre-capitalist Economic Formations" of his *A Contribution to the Critique of Political Economy*. This latter work has been translated into Chinese and included in Volume 46, Part I, of *Works of Marx and Engels*, Chinese edition. In its publication note for this extremely important work of Marx's the publisher, the Editorial and Translation Bureau of the Works of Marx, Engels, Lenin, and Stalin under the Central Committee of the Chinese Communist Party, writes, among other things:

> *A Contribution to the Critique of Political Economy (Draft of 1857-58)* was written between October 1857 and May 1858. As the preliminary draft of *Capital*, this voluminous work of rich content occupies a special place in the history of the development of Marxism. In this draft, Marx expounded for the first time the essential points and some details of his theory of value, on the basis of which he created his doctrine of surplus value, 'the cornerstone of Marx's economic theory'.[3] It is this creation of Marx's that, together with the formulation of the materialist concept of history, made possible the development of utopian socialism into scientific socialism.
>
> In this manuscript, Marx for the first time examined in a penetrating and systematic manner commodities, labour, value, money and capital, and explained the two-fold character of commodities and labour which creates commodities, the essence and functions of money, the transformation of money into capital as well as the necessary conditions of such transformation, the origin and essence of surplus value, the forms of its transformation and the law of its movement. He thus revealed the antagonistic contradiction inherent in the capitalist mode of production and the historical trend of its development.
>
> Here, Marx again dealt with the method of political economy, and discussed the relationship between logical analyses and historical studies. He held that it was necessary to probe into the social formations both before and after capitalism so as to enrich the study of the capitalist mode of production itself. He, therefore, examined the course of development of the various forms of property from the primitive commune to those preceeding capitalism. While discussing the social formation of the future, he made a brilliant exposition of labour, the development of human qualities and the relationships between men in communist society. In his manuscript, Marx also dwelt on the decisive role of agriculture in the national economy, economy of time and its significance, the use of science and technology in production, and other questions of far-reaching importance.

In my view, this publication note gives an appropriate evaluation of Marx's work *A Contribution to the Critique of Political Economy*. And Marx himself, too, set great store by this work of his. In a letter to F. Lassalle dated November 12, 1858, that is, after the completion of the work, he said: "It is the result of 15 years of research, that is to say, of the best period of my life . . . This work is the first to give scientific expression to a view of great significance with regard to social relations."[4] Because even Marx himself regarded this work as the result of "the best period" of his life, we should all the more give serious attention to it and respect all the scientific views contained therein. The Asiatic mode of production under discussion was one of the subjects Marx expounded in detail in this work. With a view to elucidating the historical process of the emergence of capitalist relations of production and showing that the process of the primitive formation of capital was the process of the separation of the objective conditions of labour from labour itself, he made a detailed study of the various pre-capitalist forms including the Asiatic, ancient and Germanic forms of property.

This study made by Marx enables us to understand a very important question in political economy in its broad sense, namely, that not all social formations can spontaneously develop into capitalist society. Of the three pre-capitalist modes of production Marx studied, the Asiatic one did not spontaneously develop into capitalist society due to lack of conditions for the emergence of capitalist production relations. The term "Asiatic" as used by Marx here is not a geographical one, but designates a special mode of production which can exist outside Asia. In his exposition of the Asiatic form of property, Marx mentioned Mexico and Peru, which are, of course, not in Asia. Japan is part of Asia, but Marx did not regard it as belonging to the category of the Asiatic mode of production. Indeed, all the regions and countries where the Asiatic mode of production once existed did not spontaneously develop into capitalist society. To we students of political economy in its broad sense, therefore, this theory of Marx's concerning the Asiatic mode of production is a component part of the overall economic theory of such political economy. In our study of the historical process of the formation of capitalist society, we are inevitably confronted by this major question: why did feudalism in Western Europe develop into capitalism while all the regions outside it, i.e., regions described by Marx as belonging to the category of the Asiatic mode of production, did not. Involved here, therefore, is not merely a question of terminology but a theoretical question. Our knowledge of the development of the economic formations of human society as a whole would, in point of fact, be very incomplete and incorrect — and consequently there would be no integral, scientific and comprehensive Marxist materialist concept of history — if we do not pay proper attention to, and study, this theory.

Unfortunately, such a major work of Marx's dealing with the pre-captialist mode of production as *A Contribution to the Critique of Political Economy* was not published during the lifetime of Marx and Engels. Its German original was put out successively in Moscow as late as 1939-41. So Lenin did not live to read this significant work, which was still unavailable even when Stalin wrote the chapter "Dialectical and Historical Materialism" for *History of the Communist Party of the Soviet Union (Bolsheviks)* in 1938. The German edition, however, did not draw much public attention after its appearance in the Soviet Union. As far as the western world is concerned, the German edition was published in Berlin only in 1953, the Italian edition came out in 1956, and the English edition was not presented to readers until the 1960s.

In his introduction to the English edition of the pamphlet *Pre-capitalist Economic Formations* by Marx, E. J. Hobsbawm writes: "It can be said without hesitation that any Marxist historical discussion which does not take into account the present work . . . must be reconsidered in its light."[5] This is correct. In my opinion, it is nothing fortuitous that, during the 1960s, there were again heated discussions on the Asiatic mode of production among scholars of Marxist literature in the various countries. There are at least three reasons for this phenomenon. First, with the publication of Marx's *A Contribution to the Critique of Political Economy*, it has become possible to gain a rather specific understanding of the Asiatic mode of production referred to by Marx so that some hitherto unclear questions can now be clarified. For instance, some people thought that Marx had in mind primitive society when he talked about the Asiatic mode of production whereas it is clear from the newly published manuscript of Marx's that this is not the case. Marx made it explicit that there existed different forms of the primitive commune, and that they disintegrated in different ways. As a result, different social formations — feudal, ancient and oriental[6] as referred to by Marx in his *Introduction* to *A Contribution to the Critique of Political Economy* — evolved on the basis of these different forms. Of these, the oriental social formation, i.e., society based on the Asiatic mode of production, was the earliest in human history, and that is why Marx put it first in his *Preface* to *A Contribution to the Critique of Political Economy*, followed in order by ancient society and feudal society of the Middle Ages. As the first social formation appearing after primitive society, Asiatic or oriental society retained particularly obvious traces of the primitive commune, but it was not the equivalent of primitive society. This is clear when we read the following passage from Marx's *Pre-capitalist Economic Formations*:

> The communal conditions for real appropriation through labour, such as irrigation systems (very important among the Asian peoples), means of communication, etc., will then appear as the work of the higher unity — the despotic government which is poised above the lesser communities. Cities in the proper sense arise by the side of these villages only where the location is particularly favourable to external trade, or where the head of the state and his satraps exchange their revenue (the surplus product) against labour, which they expend as labour-funds.[7]

What Marx said here, of course, did not occur in primitive society. The three pre-capitalist forms of property described by Marx are listed chronologically, and he did not specify that one must suceed the other. Therefore, with regard to the history of social development, Marx if fact took a multilinear approach while Stalin's was unilinear. Both of them, of course, proceeded from the premise of the materialist concept of history and, therefore, their approaches cannot be confused with the historical pluralism of the bourgeois scholars. Since the publication of Marx's *A Contribution to the Critique of Political Economy* has made it possible to clarify many questions which had remained unsolved or which had even been comprehended incorrectly, it is fully understandable that discussions have been resumed on the Asiatic mode of production.

The second reason for such renewed interest on this particular mode of production must, as I see it, be described as one of the inevitable results of the liquidation of the personality cult of Stalin. It may be recalled that a conclusion was reached at the symposium on the Asiatic mode of production held in Leningrad in 1931, that there had been no such mode of production in history. Then those theorists who thought otherwise were criticised and even persecuted. In Section 2, Chapter Four of the *History of the C.P.S.U. (B.)* published in 1938, Stalin listed only five different modes of production, arbitrarily omitting the Asiatic mode of production referred to by Marx. As a result, this particular mode of production was regarded as a forbidden zone. Whoever talked about it would be labelled a Trotskyite or at least considered as subscribing to a Trotskyite view, which would mean disaster for anyone in the Soviet Union of the time. Nobody, however, can repress for long by whatever administrative measures the truth expounded by Marx. After the personality cult of Stalin had been done away with, E. Varga, a famous Soviet economist, came out in the 1960s with an article calling for renewed discussions in the Soviet Union of the question of the Asiatic mode of production. It won response from many scholars. This shows the relationship between such reopened discussions and the elimination of the deification of Stalin.

In my view, however, the really important reason for the revived academic exchange on the Asiatic mode of production is the requirements of contemporary revolutionary practice, for all revolutionary theories must always serve the needs of such practice. Since the 1960s various countries of the vast Third World have won independence one after another, and this constitutes the mainstream of revolution in the contemporary world. Following their political independence, these countries in Asia, Africa and Latin America have demanded economic and cultural independence. They are wholly justified in demanding that there should be some historical works dealing with questions posed by their specific conditions. On the other hand, most of the books on world history and the related theories available now may be said to centre on Western Europe. As such, they cannot meet the needs of the people of the Third World. So Marxists of the world have again taken up Marx's theory of the Asiatic mode of production, restudying it in the context of the actual historical conditions of the Asian, African, and

Latin American regions. There is nothing strange about this at all.[8]

For we students of Marxist political economy, the path the newly emerging countries of the Third World will traverse in their economic development is a new major subject of study. This necessitates an understanding of the historical past of these Asian, African and Latin American countries, especially the features of their economic development which were related to those of the Asiatic mode of production discussed by Marx. From the angle of Marxist political economy in its broad sense, we must, therefore, give adequate attention to the study of Marx's theory of the Asiatic mode of production which makes up an important part of the overall theory of such political economy.

Here I would like to state, in passing, my view regarding the question whether in their later years, i.e. from the 1870s on, Marx and Engels gave up the theory of the Asiatic mode of production. This is a new question raised in the recent worldwide discussions on such a particular mode of production. I maintain that, ever since the formation of their theory of the Asiatic mode of production, Marx and Engels never discarded it, and this was also the case in their later years. It is true that Engels did not touch upon Asia in his work *The Origin of the Family, Private Property and the State*, written in the later period of his life, but he made a point of explaining this in the book. He said: "Space does not allow us to consider the gentile institutions still exsisting in greater or lesser degree of purity among the most various savage and barbarian peoples, nor the traces of these institutions in the ancient history of the civilised peoples of Asia."[9] The "ancient world" Engels referred to in this work meant Greece and Rome and did not include Asia. As for his *Anti-Dühring* published in 1877-78, I think it propagated the theory of the Asiatic mode of production instead of renouncing it, as has been asserted by some people. To criticise Dühring's force theory, Engels expounded in this book the two ways in which classes arose in human society. One was the formation of slavery, in connection with which Engels said: "Without slavery, no Greek state, no Greek art and science; without slavery, no Roman Empire, no modern Europe either."[10] What Engels said here refers, of course, to the formation of classes and states in the West. But side by side with this, Engels pointed out another way in which the formation of classes began only with the excercise of a social function. He wrote:

> ... The excercise of a social function was everywhere the basis of political domination; ... political domination has existed for any length of time only when it discharged this, its social, function. However many the despotisms which rose and fell in Persia and India, each was fully aware that it was above all the general entrepreneur for the maintenance of irrigation throughout the river valleys, without which no agriculture was possible. It was reserved for the enlightened English to lose sight of this in India; they let the irrigation canals and sluices fall into decay, and are now at last discovering as a result of the regularly recurring famines that they have neglected the one activity which might have made their rule in India at least as legitimate as that of their predecessors.[11]

What Engels wrote here was fully in agreement with Marx's description of the Asiatic form of property mentioned previously. If Marx and Engels had given up the theory of the Asiatic mode of production in their later years, why did Engels find it necessary to talk about the two ways in which classes were formed? Wouldn't it be better, in that case, to discuss only slavery? The reason why, in his *Anti-Dühring*, Engels dwelt on the two ways of the formation of classes, i.e., of states, is that, apart from the way followed by Greece and the Roman Empire, there existed another, the Asiatic way.

Still another proof — and a most convincing one at that — of the fact that Marx and Engels never changed their theory of the Asiatic mode of production is Volume

III of *Capital*. Examining pre-capitalist ground rent, Marx said:

> Should the direct producers not be confronted by a private landowner, but rather, as in Asia, under direct subordination to a state which stands over them as their landlord and simultaneously as sovereign, then rent and taxes coincide, or rather, there exists no tax which differs from this form of ground rent. Under such circumstances, there need exist no stronger political or economic pressure than that common to all subjection to that state. The state is then the supreme lord. Sovereignty here consists in the ownership of land concentrated on a national scale. But, on the other hand, no private ownership of land exists, although there is both private and common possession and use of land.[12]

The special form of ground rent referred to by Marx was precisely that existing under "oriental despotism", discussed in the section on the Asiatic form of property. The two completely agreed in content. This shows that the theory of the Asiatic mode of production was a consistent theory created by Marx and Engels, a theory which they continued to uphold in their later years. Of course, we should note here that it was Richard Jones of the school of classical political economy, and not Marx, who first discovered the existence of this form of ground rent in history. Jones called it "Ryot". How Marx critically inherited Jones' theory on this subject can be seen from his *Theories of Surplus Value*,[13] so we will not go deep into it here. What I want to stress is that, since they continued to publicise their theory of the Asiatic mode of production in such important works of their later years as *Anti-Dühring* and Volume III of *Capital*, how can anyone say that they changed their stand on this question towards the closing periods of their lifetimes?

II. The significance of the theory of the Asiatic mode of production for the study of world history and Chinese history

We have seen the significance of Marx's theory of the

Asiatic mode of production from the angle of political economy in its broad sense, i.e., from the angle of studying how pre-capitalist societies developed into capitalist society. Now we would like to probe into the question whether or not the oriental or Asiatic society, whether the ancient oriental or Asiatic states based on the Asiatic mode of production as referred to by Marx — whether or not they existed at some specific stage of human history. If they existed, then how did they develop? What changes did they undergo? Were there any particular laws governing their development? Now let me state my personal view on these questions.

Let us start with world history. As I see it, the first group of states that appeared in human history was the ancient oriental states of the Copper Age and/or the Bronze Age, i.e., those represented by Egypt and Babylonia. This means that the oriental society and oriental states discussed by Marx were objective realities in history. Generally speaking, these states conformed to the economic characteristics described in Marx's classical work *Pre-capitalist Economic Formations*. And these characteristics are as follows:

1. There existed landownership by the village commune and by the state, and these forms of ownership were associated with the farming system based on artificial irrigation. The sovereigns who had unlimited powers were the supreme or sole owners of land in their states.

2. The main producers in these states were members of the village communes, i.e., the peasants. The productive forces were of an extremely low level because the production implements of the Bronze Age remained practically the same as those of the Neolithic Age.

3. The despotic governments poised above the small village communes depended on tribute — the surplus labour of the peasants of these communes or their

surplus products — for existence. These governments which controlled land and water resources as well as handicrafts and commerce were politically absolutist.

4. As the basis of such absolutism, the village communes were self-sufficient economic organisations combining handicrafts and agriculture. They became "entirely self-sustaining" and contained within themselves "all conditions of production and surplus production".[14] Thus they had a great vitality and were resurgent.

5. The slaves within these states were employed mainly in non-productive household duties.

The ancient states in China also came into being in the Copper Age and/or Bronze Age. Consequently, I have concluded from my research that China should belong to the same type of ancient oriental states as Egypt and Babylonia, i.e., ancient oriental states of the Asiatic type. A comparison of ancient China with ancient Egypt and Babylonia, however, shows two salient points. The first concerns the use of slaves. While in ancient Egypt and Babylonia slaves were used mainly in nonproductive household chores, in ancient China — at least during the Western Zhou Dynasty (c. 11th century-770 BC) — they were employed in productive undertakings apart from housework in families of the clan nobles. Since the slaves were former prisoners of war or criminals, they were owned by the state and clan nobility. They laboured on opening up mountain and forest areas and on the construction of irrigation channels and roads as well as other onerous tasks including bronze casting. Chronologically, not many of the slaves of the Yin Dynasty[15] were used in production because most of them served as human sacrifices or were buried alive with their dead masters as funerary objects. This can be seen from the mass of human bones excavated in post-liberation years from tombs of that period. By the subsequent Zhou Dynasty (c. 11th century-221 BC), fewer and fewer slaves were slaughtered to serve as funerary objects, which tells us that they were now used for other puposes. Nevertheless, production in this period was generally carried on by members of the village communes as before.

The second outstanding point concerns the village commune system. As China covered a much wider territory than that of Egypt and Babylonia, it had more clans; and as the level of productive forces varied greatly from region to region, the commune system, or what is known in history as the *jingtian* ("well field") system (cultivation of communal land in turns), of ancient China was a rather complicated affair. With a diverse content, it developed unevenly in different regions. Our current research, however, has led us to believe that it probably had the following four essential aspects:

1. The supreme landowner in a state was the king or the "Son of Heaven". Since the clan nobility had already set up the patriarchal and fief systems for safeguarding and consolidating its rule, land and population were owned level by level according to the heirarchy of the nobles. (Closely related to each other, the patriarchal system and fief system first appeared in the Shang Dynasty and became relatively perfect by the Western Zhou Dynasty.) At the time, all land was within the domain of a state, and this formed the basis of the rule of a patriarchal clan, or its economic basis. All nobles, from the "Son of Heaven" down to his ministers, lived on tribute from the village communes.

2. Within the commune itself, land was divided into "communal land" and "private land". The first was tilled collectively by commune members to support rulers of the clan while the second — the limited share a commune member received through distribution — was to be returned to the commune for unified use after a fixed period of time.

3. Generally speaking, land of the *jingtian* system was cultivated collectively by two-man teams.

4. Such land was square in shape, and this in reality represented a given stage in the development of agricultural production. Square land also existed in occidental society, the system being known as the "square plot system" in Europe and, more specifically, "Celtic field system" in England. This system collapsed in Europe when iron ploughs began to be used, and the same happened to China's *jingtian* system during the Warring States Period (475-221 BC) when land cultivation by iron ploughs became widespread. It is nothing strange at all that square land first appeared during the Yin and Western Zhou periods when *lei* and *si* (two primitive forms of wooden plough) were in use.

Judging from these four essential aspects — and chiefly the first and the second — of the *jingtian* system, I am of the opinion that this system was the Asiatic type of land-ownership referred to by Marx, in fact land-ownership by clan nobles in an ancient oriental state of the Bronze Age. What was characteristic of ancient China was that the patriarchal system which had evolved out of primitive kinship organisations was combined with such land-ownership to become a particular system — a land system as well as a political and economic one — suited to the needs of the dictatorship by clan nobility. Such a system was absent in other ancient oriental states of the Bronze Age, for the fiefs in ancient Egypt and Babylonia were not closely related to the patriarchal system. Hence what has been described is a salient feature of China as an ancient oriental state.

By the Iron Age, changes in the productive forces led to corresponding changes in relations of production. But history shows that the superstructure of the ancient oriental states of the Bronze Age presented a formidable obstacle to the new productive forces (for instance, the widespead use of iron implements). Ancient Egypt was a case in point. Four centuries after its entry into the Iron Age, its smiths were still using the clumsy hand tools of the Bronze Age while their Greek counterparts of the same peroid had extensively adopted iron implements.[16] It is thus clear that not all the oriental states of the Bronze Age underwent timely, corresponding changes when new productive forces and new production relations had emerged in society. Obviously, after they had entered the Iron Age, such oriental states of the Bronze Age as ancient Egypt and those in Mesopotamia were conquered by others before they could conduct any reforms. China was, therefore, truly a rare example in world history, for, as an ancient oriental state of the Bronze Age, it went through corresponding changes after entering the Iron Age and then became a despotic *fengjian*[17] state of the Asiatic type. Research proves that China advanced from the use of wooden ploughs (*lei* and *si*) to that of ox-drawn iron ploughs in the Warring States Period, before which iron implements were still not widely adopted and those in use were only small household ironware and small farm tools of iron. It is, of course, nothing accidental that China carried out reforms in the Warring States Period, the State of Qin being the first to succeed in this respect. This was due to the uneven political and economic development in the various regions and the relative weakness of the conservative clan nobility of Qin. These factors enabled Qin to institute some reforms which were more drastic than those in some other advanced states. (Nevertheless, Shang Yang, architect of the reforms, was killed by the nobles who took retaliatory measures against him after the death of Duke Xiao, the Qin ruler who ordered the carrying out of these reforms.) Because Qin abolished the *jingtian* system, extended help to the small peasants and adopted advanced political and economic systems to make production relations conform to the character of the new productive forces, production developed markedly, paving the way for Shilhuangdi (the First Emperor) of the Qin Dynasty (221-207 BC) to unify the whole of China and establish a centralised *fengjian* empire of the Asiatic type.

Having entered the *fengjian* period earlier than its counterparts in the world, China should also have developed into a capitalist country at an earlier date. But this was not the case, the reasons for which should be sought in connection with Marx's theory of the Asiatic mode of production. Compared with the feudal society of Western Europe, Chinese *fengjian* society since the Qin and Han (221 BC-AD 220) dynasties possessed the following prominent features of the Asiatic type:

1. China had private land-ownership as well as state land-ownership characteristic of a *fengjian* society. The sovereign was the biggest and supreme landlord in the whole *fengjian* state who ruled over all its people and made them carry out all kinds of *fengjian* obligations to him.

2. On the basis of landownership by the *fengjian* state, the imperial court controlled not only its land and water resources but also its most important handicraft and commercial enterprises (this latter aspect can be seen, among other things, from the state monopoly of salt and iron).

3. In Chinese *fengjian* society, land could be bought and sold. Since Chinese landed capital was closely bound up with merchant and usurer's capital, the following situation described by Marx in *Capital* did not occur in China: "As a matter of history, capital, as opposed to landed property, invariably takes the form at first of money; it appears as moneyed wealth, as the capital of the merchant and of the usurer."[18]

4. In *fengjian* China, remnant slavery existed for quite a long time, and this is the case as regards, in

particular, slaves reduced to their status as such by debts and slaves who were formerly criminals. There is also the factor of the prolonged existence of the patriarchal clan system. Thus slave exploitation and clan patriarchy combined to form a most important form of exploitation and domination in Chinese *fengjian* society. The working people suffered extremely cruel exploitation.

5. Lack of a typical manorial economy and serfs explains why there were no free cities in Chinese *fengjian* society. The relationship between town and country was completely different from that in Europe. Because of a lack of a bourgeoisie in Chinese cities, which was a powerful force in the development of private capitalism, it was the landlords and bureaucrats who held sway there.

6. The principal economic pillar of Chinese *fengjian* society was small-peasant economy in the vast countryside, including that of the owner peasants and tenants. Agriculture and handicrafts were inseparably linked to each other to form the basis of a natural economy, thus impeding the development of a commodity economy in China. Whatever commodity production (e.g., manufacture of silks and porcelain) prospered to a fair extent in *fengjian* China, the society basically served the consumption needs of the bureaucrats and landlords.

These distinct features of China's *fengjian* society, in comparison with Europe, are in fact the reasons why Chinese society developed at an especially slow speed after the Qin and Han dynasties instead of growing into capitalism fairly rapidly as West European feudalism did. And some of these features were exactly carried over from, and evolved out of, the socio-economic features of the ancient orient. For instance, state ownership in Chinese *fengjian* society was obviously a continuation of, and an advance on, that in the Yin and

Western Zhou dynasties. Although private landlords had appeared in China since the Warring States, Qin and Han periods, the situation remained as in the past with respect to the state functioning as the supreme landlord. The owner peasants engaged in individual production were the most important direct producers in the country. Essentially tenants of the *fengjian* state, they bore the bulk of the land tribute and the taxes paid to it. This is totally different from Western European feudal society where serfs were the chief producers. For another thing, the patriarchal system, which existed throughout Chinese *fengjian* society, was also inherited from and developed out of patriarchy in ancient times. Such close integration of *fengjian*-ism with patriarchy was unknown in feudal society of Western Europe. Comrade Mao Zedong paid great attention to this point. He called it clan authority, which was combined with the political authority, the religious authority and the authority of the husband as the "embodiment of the whole feudal (*fengjian*)-patriachal system and ideology", as "the four thick ropes binding the Chinese people, particularly the peasants".[19] Precisely because the ancient, backward Asiatic mode of production existed to a great extent, the development of Chinese *fengjian* society could not but be considerably hindered.

Moreover, there were many powerful private landlords in China's *fengjian* dynasties. Enjoying various *fengjian* privileges, they could exploit the peasants at will without contributing corvee to the state and without paying taxes (or they paid only little taxes). Under such circumstances, the small peasants suffering from the double burden of land tribute and taxes and free labour were liable to lose their land and thus became tenants or dependent peasants at the mercy of the powerful private landlords. Such concentration of land sharpened the two types of contradiction existing in Chinese *fengjian* society: the contradiction between the public and private interests (between the central government and the local *fengjian* forces, or between the state and the influential landlords) and the contradiction between the ownership of land and its use.

The situation concerning the first type of contradiction was as follows: Since the small peasants in Chinese *fengjian* society paid most of the land tribute and taxes and supplied most of the corvee services, their increasingly reduced number through land annexation meant less and less revenue directly accruing to the imperial treasury. This was unfavourable for the *fengjian* dynasty as a whole because, as a centralised despotic state of the Asiatic type, it had to fulfil certain social and economic functions such as coping with the invasion by the nomadic peoples and launching water control and irrigation projects, all of which must be funded by state revenue. The prosperity of such a *fengjian* state was evidently determined by two factors. One is that the total sum of land rent and tribute and taxes that it collected from the direct producers could not exceed that needed for reproduction. The other is that there must be sufficient revenue to finance the private enjoyment of the ruling class, and that an appropriate portion of state revenue must be used to fund the carrrying out of its social and economic functions. But here lay the inner contradiction of Chinese *fengjian* despotism: On the one hand, the dynasty could not but depend on the masses of small peasants for productive undertakings. On the other, the privileged private landlords unavoidably increased the burdens of the small peasants through rent, causing the step-by-step annexation of their land and thereby reducing the state revenue.

At the same time, since such land annexation affected only the ownership of private land and not the right of its use, it aggravated another contradiction in Chinese *fengjian* society, namely, contradiction between the ownership of land and its use. As it is, these two aspects developed in opposite directions in Chinese history. That is why, while the ownership of private land tended to concentrate in the hands of a small number of big private landlords, its use became increasingly scattered, for otherwise the landlords could not rent it out. The situation of such land parcels used in a scattered way was, in Marx's words, actually like this: "Progressive deterioration of conditions of production and increased prices of means of production — an inevitable law of proprietorship of parcels. Calamity of seasonal abundance for this mode of production."[20] Hence, far from improving, the conditions of the small peasants as the principal producers in successive dynasties grew worse and worse.

From what has been described above, we can say that, when the revenue of the *fengjian* court had diminished more and more because of the growth of the power of the privileged big landlords, in other words, when the central government could no longer finance the water control projects and arms build-up, and when rent and taxes had become so exorbitant that most of the direct producers (the peasants) lost their land and could no longer survive on it — when things had reached this point, the *fengjian* dynasty would soon be overthrown by the peasant masses or conquered by the nomadic peoples outside its domain. In this way, the intrinsic contradiction of the land system in Chinese *fengjian* society eventually developed into the contradiction between the landlord class (the class of landowners) and the peasantry (the class of actual land users). And this explains the intermittent peasant uprisings in the *fengjian* period, resulting in the replacement of one dynasty by another.

Peasant uprisings and peasant wars in Chinese *fengjian* society played an exceedingly important role in furthering historical progress. As Comrade Mao Zedong pointed out in his article *The Chinese Revolution and the Chinese Communist Party*, "the scale of peasant uprisings and peasant wars in Chinese history has no parallel anywhere else. The class struggles of the peasants, the peasant uprisings and peasant wars constituted the real motive force of historical development in Chinese feudal *(fengjian)* society."[21] In the context of the changing economic conditions under Chinese *fengjian*-ism, the ruling class was often compelled by such uprisings and wars to adopt various land and tax systems to readjust the prevailing relations of production and make them suit the developing productive forces. The land system developed from the reclamation of wasteland by garrison troops or peasants (as practiced in the Han Dynasty and the State of Wei, 220-265) to the limited landholding by nobles (as in the Jin Dynasty, 265-420), to land equalisation (as in the Tang Dynasty, 618-907) and to the post Tang system largely similar to the manorial system in the West. Concerning the tax system, the development was clear from the Han Dynasty's land rent, poll tax and payment for exemption from military service to the Tang Dynasty's system combining rent, labour services and tax in kind, to its subsequent two-tax system (with taxes fixed in proportion to the size of the payer's property and paid in cash twice a year — in summer and autumn) and then to the Ming Dynasty's "One Whip Law" which had the various taxes and corvee services merged into a single tax payable in cash. We need not explain these complicated measures in detail, but the transition from one to another indicated a trend of development, i.e., along with the advance of history, private land-ownership in *fengjian* society developed at the expense of the state land-ownership. The control of the imperial court over the people passed more and more from direct control of the person and demand for unpaid labour to extraction of taxes, enabling commodities and money to play an ever-increasing role in the economy. It may be said that this was a trend in the direction of capitalism. China was, after all, a state of the Asiatic type where the development of capitalism was obstructed by forces so powerful that, prior to the Opium War of 1840-42, there were as yet no such capitalist productive forces and production relations in Chinese *fengjian* society as those obtaining in the feudal society of Western Europe. Thus China did not develop into a capitalist society.[22]

A study of the historical development of China in comparison with that of the Western world shows that Marx's theory of the Asiatic mode of production was well founded, and that China itself furnishes a best proof of it. Now the question is: will recognition of China's historical development as the development of the Asiatic, i.e., recognition of Marx's theory of the Asiatic mode of production — will this provide the Western imperialists with a "theoretical" weapon for their invasion against the backward oriental nations? It should be admitted that there were — and are — really some reactionaries who utilised this theory of Marx's to apologise for such invasion, and even to oppose Marx's theory of the dictatorship of the proletariat. An example of the former case was the hired scribblers serving the Japanese militarists during China's War of Resistance Against Japan (1937-45). They did all they could to propagate the "progressive nature" of Japanese imperialism's attempt to conquer China, trying to provide a "theoretical" basis for its aggressive policy aimed at subjugating the Chinese nation. An example of the latter case is K. A. Wittfogel, an American Sinologist who wrote a book, *Oriental Despotism*, to oppose our theory of the dictatorship of the proletariat.

We must definitely criticise and repudiate all "theories" designed to oppose our revolution and proletarian dictatorship. But we must never negate

Marx's scientific theory of the Asiatic mode of production on account of our opposing and criticising such fallacies. According to Marx's viewpoint, a socio-economic formation is an objective historical process. To recognise and understand this process does not mean that we should always remain powerless before it. On the contrary. We should take proper, revolutionary actions on the basis of our correct understanding of the features of such historical process. Take our own country as an example. The fact that China did not spontaneously develop into a capitalist society does not mean that we can never make our motherland a modern state. Historical development has proved that even such an ancient country as China — a typical ancient state belonging to the category of the Asiatic mode of production — can, in a relatively short historical period, embark on the broad path of socialist modernisation through the new democratic revolution and the socialist revolution, provided that there is the correct leadership of the Chinese Communist Party. The Chinese revolution succeeded only with the correct understanding of the characteristics of Chinese society on the part of the older generation of proletarian revolutionaries headed by Comrade Mao Zedong, only with the birth of Mao Zedong Thought and the renunciation of the so-called "revolutionary line" imposed on us at the time by the Third International. Now that China is building socialism in its own way which conforms to its actual conditions, the study of Marx's theory of the Asiatic mode of production will do much good to our modernisation of the country's agriculture, industry, national defence and science and technology. That is because historical development itself is dialectical, and what is backward in one period may become an advanced element in the next. In ancient times, Western Europe lagged behind China in economic development, but it went ahead of us in the capitalist period. China has its backward side at present, for instance, the backward conditions in its countryside, especially the vestiges of the ancient village commune still found in some rural areas inhabited by certain minority nationalities. In the light of what Marx said in his reply to V. I. Zasulich, however, such backward phenomena can become an element in the rebirth of Chinese society and an advantageous element as compared with countries still under the capitalist yoke.[23] Therefore, we should, again as Marx taught, not be particularly afraid of the term "Asiatic". On the contrary. We should, in my view, intensify our study of Marx's theory of the Asiatic mode of production and endeavour to prove its correctness by China's own practice.

This is my understanding of the significance of the theory of the Asiatic mode of production for the study of Chinese history as well as world history. With regard to its significance in other respects, such as for the study of contemporary world economy, that belongs to another subject which I will not talk about here.

1. Engels, *Anti-Dühring*, Foreign Languages Press, Beijing, 1976, p.191.
2. *Ibid.*, p.192.
3. Lenin, *The Three Sources and Three Component Parts of Marxism*, FLP, Beijing, 1978, p.71.
4. Marx and Engels, *Works*, Russian edition, Vol. 29.
5. Marx, *Pre-capitalist Economic Formations*, International Publishers, New York, 1980, p.10.
6. Here, Marx arranged the three different social formations in a reverse chronological order. — *Wu.*
7. *Ibid.*, pp.70-71.
8. There should be special articles to introduce the results of the discussions on the Asiatic mode of production that have been held in the various countries. What I would like to point out here is that some Marxists of the Third World, Samir Amin of Egypt for one, are particularly interested in this question. It is worthwhile to translate and publish their works on the Asiatic mode of production. — *Wu.*

THE ASIATIC MODE OF PRODUCTION IN HISTORY

9. *The Origin of the Family, Private Property and the State*, FLP, Beijing, 1978, p.156.
10. *Anti-Dühring*, FLP, Beijing, 1976, p.231.
11. *Ibid.*, p.230.
12. Marx, *Capital*, Foreign Languages Publishing House, Moscow, 1959, Vol. III, pp.771-2.
13. Cf. Marx, *Theories of Surplus Value*, Progress Publishers, Moscow, 1971, Part III, Chapter, XXIV.
14. Marx, *Pre-capitalist Economic Formations*, International Publishers, New York, 1980, p.70.
15. The Shang Dynasty (c. 16th-11th century BC) was also called Yin after King Pan Geng moved its capital to Yin (in the present-day Henan Province) in the 14th century BC — *Translator*.
16. Cf. V. Gordon Childe, *History*, Cobbett Press, London, 1947, p.73.
17. In his writings, Comrade Mao Zedong made a fully correct analysis of Chinese *fengjian* society. Although the term *fengjian* here is usually translated into "feudal", Chinese *fengjian*-ism is not the equivalent of feudalism in English, for actually the latter refers to what was described by Marx as the Germanic form of property in Western Europe while the former actually refers to the advanced stage of what was described by Marx as the Asiatic form of property. That is why we prefer the phonetic transliteration *fengjian* to the customary translation "feudal". — *Wu*.
18. *Capital*, Progress Publishers, Moscow, 1965, Vol. I, p.146.
19. "Report on an investigation of the Peasant Movement in Hunan". *Selected Works of Mao Zedong*, FLP, Beijing, 1975, Vol. I, p.44.
20. *Capital*, FLPH, Moscow, 1959, Vol. III. P.787.
21. *Selected Works of Mao Zedong*, FLP, Beijing, 1975, Vol. II, p.308.
22. For the development of Chinese fengjian society, may I refer readers to my work *Outline of Chinese Slave Economy and "Fengjian" Economy*, Chinese edition, Sanlian Bookstore, Beijing, 1963. — *Wu*.
23. "First Draft of a Reply to V. I. Zasulich", Marx and Engels, *Works*, Russian edition, Vol. 19.

III

Is Humanism Revisionism?

Ru Xin

One day in 1979, a veteran revolutionary and famous poet whom I hold in high esteem, told me in all seriousness: "In the decade of the fascist dictatorship of Lin Biao and the Gang of Four,[1] I witnessed their appalling atrocities that were utterly inhuman and yet decked out by 'doubly revolutionary' phrases. I was so shocked that I vowed to myself that I would not take part in the criticism of humanism any more." He said this with profound emotion, which he failed to contain. His words were thought-provoking and rekindled the doubts that have been buried deep in me for all these years. I felt compelled to make a fresh study of the question of humanism.

I

Everybody knows that we regard practice as the sole criterion for testing truth. During the past two decades we have launched repeated mass criticisms of humanism, labelling it as revisionism. Their purpose was undoubtedly good, for they were meant to oppose revisionism and defend the purity of Marxism. Contrary to our wishes, however, we got the opposite results from such criticisms which led to the affirmation of medieval inhumanity. This was due to one-sided recognition and the simplified way of our thinking. We have a bitter lesson to draw in this respect: in theory, far from adding to the lustre of Marxism, our criticism of humanism distorted its true spirit. In practice, such criticism had evil consequences because it virtually encouraged the wide perpetration, under "revolutionary" banners, of diverse unlawful acts contrary to the basic norms of humanism. Facts pose a serious question to us: what, after all, is the proper relationship between Marxism and humanism? It is theoretically tenable to regard humanism as revisionism?

One of the most important arguments in the criticism of humanism had been that Marxism and humanism represent two world outlooks that are absolutely opposed to and incompatible with each other. This logic necessarily led to the conclusion that any attempt to link Marxism with humanism means "revisionism" and "misrepresentation" of Marxism.

The point at issue is: is it true that Marxism and humanism are absolutely opposed to and incompatible with each other?

As everybody knows, humanism has always been understood in two senses, the broad and the narrow. In a narrow sense, humanism refers to the intellectual and cultural movement waged during the Renaissance by the emerging European bourgeoisie against feudalism and theology. In a broad sense, humanism embraces the ideas and views that, generally speaking, stand for human dignity, rights and liberties, man's value and his fully free development, etc. Obviously, when we criticised humanism and labelled it revisionism, we had in mind not humanism in a narrow sense, not some specific school of thought prevalent at a certain historical stage, but humanism in the broad sense. In our present discussion of the relationship between Marxism and humanism, we aim, of course, not at an assessment of some school of thought that had long ago become a thing of the past, but at achieving a correct understanding of what approach Marxism should take towards a series of questions concerning man that arise in real life.

Humanist ideas may express themselves in different ways, and people with such ideas may belong to different classes and political groupings; they may have vastly different, and even sharply contradicting views on certain questions. That is why we can hardly regard humanism as a world outlook in the proper sense of the term; we can only take it as representing a viewpoint and a trend of thought on the status, role and future of man in this world of ours. To put it plainly, humanism is a belief that stands for treating man as such. The supreme objective of man is man himself, so is the value of man. All views and acts contrary to this, such as denying the independent value of man, debasing his status and regarding him as less than man (regarding him as a "talking tool", as "a plaything in the hands of God", as a commodity that can be bought or sold at will or as a means of producing surplus value, advocating that "man should despise himself", and even torturing and murdering man cold-bloodedly in the name of "revolution") — all these views and acts are in conflict with humanism. In point of fact, we can hardly evade the question of the value of man. When it comes to this question, we have to choose between humanism and anti-humanism of all descriptions.

The famous French existentialist philosopher J. P. Sartre criticised Marxism as having "submerged man in concepts", failed to study the living man and thus become "non-humanism". This, he said, was responsible for the stagnation of Marxism. He, therefore, proposed "restoring man to Marxism". (See J.P. Sartre, *Critique de la raison dialectique* (*Critique of Dialectical Reason*).) Ungrounded and unjust, his criticism revealed a gross misunderstanding of Marxism. If there are really some Marxists or self-styled Marxists who neglected the question of man and thus caused a "stagnation" of Marxist theory, they are themselves to blame. As for Marxism itself, far from neglecting the question of man, it invariably takes the solution of human problems as its point of departure and central task.

When he formulated his own revolutionary theory as a challenge to the old world as a whole, Marx solemnly declared: "Theory is capable of gripping the masses as soon as it demonstrates *ad hominem*, and it demonstrates *ad hominem* as soon as it becomes radical. To be radical is to grasp the root of the matter. But for man the root is man himself." He also pointed out that the criticism of modern politico-social reality should be elevated to "truly human problems". And, in the final analysis, "the only *practically* possible liberation of Germany is liberation that proceeds from the standpoint of *the* theory which proclaims man to be the highest being for man".[2] We may say that, from the very day of its birth, Marxism has taken the emancipation of man as its supreme objective? So how can one say that there is no place for man in Marxist theory?

One of the reasons why Marxism can make a profound and effective criticism of the reality of capitalist society is precisely that it does not limit itself to exposure and condemnation of the maladies and crimes of the capitalist social system. Proceeding from a much higher plane by raising "truly human problems", it scientifically expounds the capitalist ruin of man and all the harmful consequences of capitalism for man's further development, and analyses the objective conditions that gave rise to such an anti-humanistic character of the capitalist system. Marx's *Economic and*

Philosophic Manuscripts of 1844 provides a clear example in this connection. In it Marx forcefully pointed out that capitalist society manifests itself as the complete loss of man because "the *devaluation* of the world of men is in direct proportion to the *increasing value* of the world of things".[3] The estrangement of man has reached the height of absurdity, for the worker has become completely bonded to the object labour produces and is dominated by a non-human force. The worker becomes all the poorer, the more wealth he produces; he becomes an ever cheaper commodity, the more commodities he creates; labour produces beauty, but the worker becomes deformed, labour produces intelligence, but the worker is rewarded with stupidity, cretinism. Such estrangement is manifested not only in the result but in the act of production, within the producing activity itself. Creative labour, which is a human characteristic that distinguishes man from the other animals and through which he achieves a free and overall development of himself, is now replaced by estranged labour. To the worker labour has become a suffering, for in his work he does not affirm but denies himself, he does not freely develop his physical and mental energy but mortifies his body and ruins his mind. As a result, the worker feels himself freely active only in his animal functions (eating, drinking, procreating, etc.); and in his human functions, i.e., in the labour-process, he no longer feels himself to be anything but an animal. Hence this abnormal reversal of things: "What is animal becomes human and what is human becomes animal."[4] The character of human beings should have been free, conscious activity, but now their activity has been relegated to merely a means of maintaining their physical existence. Thus a man has lost himself, has lost his value as man, and become "a *mentally* and physically *dehumanised* being".[5]

What has been described above shows that the crime

of capitalism lies not merely in one class oppressing and exploiting another, but all the more in its causing the loss and enslavement of mankind as a whole. Precisely because of this, the aim of communist revolution should not be restricted to the overthrow of the capitalist system and the emancipation of the working class from the rule of the capitalists; it should be the emancipation of the whole of mankind. And precisely because of this, Marx, when outlining the prospects of communism, raised the question of "the return of man to himself". He described communism as "the *positive* transcendence of *private property* as *human self-estrangement*", and, therefore, as "the real *appropriation* of the *human* essence by and for man", and as "the complete return accomplished consciously and embracing the entire wealth of previous development".[6] Marx also pointed out emphatically that communism is no loss of man's essential powers born to the realm of objectivity, not a returning in poverty to primitive simplicity, but "the actual realisation for man of man's essence and of his essence a something real".[7]

II

If we adopt a scientific and objective, instead of a biased, attitude, we shall have to admit that, from the time Marx embarked on his career as a communist, he concerned himself most with the analysis of man and the prospects of the development of man in the future communist society. He displayed the consistent humanist spirit of giving first place to the value of man. In fact, Marx himself made it clear that "communism ... as fully developed naturalism, equals humanism",[8] and that "communism is humanism mediated with itself through the supersession of private property".[9] With the best of intentions, some of our comrades try to draw a clear line between Marxism and humanism, and keep silent on these of Marx's statements. This is absolutely unnecessary, for we need not worry about our wallowing in the mire with some other Western bourgeois "Marxologists". Their real mistake lies not in the fact that they regard Marx, whose views were outlined in his *Economic and Philosophic Manuscripts of 1844*, as humanist; their real mistake lies in the following: 1) They set the young Marx against the ideologically mature Marx, alleging that the Marx of latter years "renounced" the humanist ideas of the young Marx. 2) They lump together Marxist humanism and bourgeois humanism of the past, obliterating the differences in principle between them.

Marx's thinking went through a process of development, and the young Marx was naturally different from the ideologically mature Marx. The point is how to look at and appraise such a difference. Some comrades think that, since the young Marx had not yet become a Marxist due to Feuerbach's negative influence, his formulations on the questions of man and humanism as contained in the *Economic and Philosophic Manuscripts of 1844* were not Marxist, but represented the remnant influence of the anthropological philosophy of Feuerbach. This view summarily excludes young Marx's exceptionally profound ideas on the question of man from the scope of Marxist theory, and denies the continuity and inner connections between the ideas included in these manuscripts and Marx's more mature ideas. In fact, such a view adds to the mistake of setting the young Marx against the ideologically mature Marx.

In examining the development of Marx's thinking, we must never forget that he did not go through the school of Hegel and Feuerbach for nothing. Hegel tried to replace the cult of God with the cult of reason, and the reason and Absolute Idea as he enunciated them were but the abstraction of thought divorced from concrete man. Indeed, there was in him a real "submerging" of man "in concepts". Having criticised Hegel's idealist mistake, Feuerbach did his best to replace abstract reason with real living man. But he could not find a way out of the realm of abstraction into that of living reality. Man as he understood him was not man living in a concrete socio-historical environment and in the context of class relations; such man was, therefore, still abstract man. Only Marx succeeded in finding the correct point of departure, the real man, by means of criticism of Hegel and Feuerbach. Engels said: " ... The step Feuerbach did not take had to be taken. The cult of abstract man, which formed the kernel of Feuerbach's new religion, had to be replaced by the science of real men and of their historical development. This further development of Feuerbach's standpoint beyond Feuerbach was inaugurated by Marx in 1845 in *The Holy Family*."[10]

Please note that it is the *"further development* of Feuerbach's standpoint *beyond* Feuerbach", instead of summarily discarding it. On no account did the criticism of Feuerbach by the founders of Marxism mean the discarding of man and returning to Hegel's "submerging" of man "in concepts"; it meant proceeding from abstract man to real man. Feuerbach was not wrong in taking man as the point of departure; the point is that man as he understood him was too abstract, and that he took the essence of man to be "abstraction inherent in each single individual" and "an inner, mute, general character which unites the many individuals *in a natural way*".[11] Consequently, the Feuerbach-type humanism based on such abstraction could only be of a fantastic character (for example, its preachings on love). Generally speaking, this was a limitation insurmountable for all types of humanism prior to Marxism. It is Marx who, for the first time, understood the essence of men as "the ensemble of the social relations".[12] Thus the real living man, man of flesh and blood, appeared before us. From the writings of the young Marx, we can already see his initial probe into the question of real man conducted independently of Feuerbach. His latter works written when he had become ideologically mature were precisely the bountiful fruit of such an early probe. Along with the maturing of his thinking, Marx gained a deeper and deeper understanding of real man and found an increasingly scientific solution to human problems. If this is a fact, how can we say that Marx "renounced" his early ideas of humanism?

The two great discoveries, i.e., the materialist conception of history and surplus value, marked the full maturity of Marx's thinking. The materialist conception of history explains the objective law of the historical development of human society, while the theories of surplus value reveal the secret of exploitation of man by man under the capitalist mode of production. Instead of liquidating or weakening Marx's humanism, these epoch-making discoveries provided it with a truly scientific basis, thus enabling it to be consolidated. It is precisely thanks to these discoveries that people, for the first time in history, got a clear idea of man's social essence and of how a concrete analysis of man should be made. As a result, the emancipation of man ceased to be merely a beautiful vision in the minds of utopians: it had become the subject of precise, scientific study. Strictly speaking, it is only with the birth of Marxism that the study of man became a genuine science. A comparison between Marx's early works with those written after he had become ideologically mature shows that human problems had always been at the centre of his attention, and that he had been invariably and deeply concerned with the status and destiny of man. It is only that the young Marx had not yet acquired an adequate knowledge of the inevitable historical trend and objective law of the development of human society. He came to a more and more concrete and precise understanding of all this with the passage of time, and it thus became possible for him to give a scientific exposition of the true road of the emancipation of mankind, presenting it as a practical revolutionary programme.

Now let us cite a few examples from some of the universally acknowledged Marxist works in order to illustrate the continuity and development of Marx's ideas of humanism described above.

1. It is stated in *The Holy Family* that the propertied class and the proletariat present the same human self-estrangement. The proletariat is necessarily driven to indignation because it sees in such self-estrangement "the reality of an inhuman existence" and because there is "the contradiction between its human nature and its condition of life, which is the outright, resolute and comprehensive negation of that nature". To emancipate itself, the proletariat has to abolish "*all* the inhuman conditions of life of society today which are summed up in its own situation".[13]

2. Discussing the historical inevitability of the emergence of private property and of the division of labour and their consequences on men, *The German Ideology* says that division of labour will be abolished only when the productive forces have grown to such an extent that private property and the division of labour become fetters on them. The abolition of private property presupposes the free development of individuals, and communist revolution is "a general condition for their free development". Only in communist society will "the genuine and free development of individuals"[14] cease to be a mere phrase.

3. *The Communist Manifesto* says that the proletariat must make itself the ruling class, sweep away the old conditions of production and at the same time eliminate the conditions for the existence of class antagonisms and

abolish all classes. In place of the old bourgeois society with its class antagonisms, "we shall have an association, in which the free development of each is the condition for the free development of all".[15]

4. In his *Anti-Dühring*, a work which won the full approval of Marx, Engels dealt with the change of man's status in the future society. He wrote that the seizure of the means of production by society eliminates the domination of the product over the producer and the anarchy of social production is replaced by consciously planned organisation. At this point, "man finally separates in a certain sense from the animal kingdom and . . . he passes from animal conditions of existence to really human ones".[16] For the first time, humanity becomes the real conscious master of nature. The objective extraneous forces which have hitherto dominated history now pass under the control of man. It is only from this point that man will himself fully consciously make his own history. This Engels called "humanity's leap from the realm of necessity into the realm of freedom".[17]

5. Marx also discussed, in his *Capital*, Volume III, the question of man's leap from the realm of necessity into the realm of freedom, maintaining that the heart of the matter lies in the shortening of the working day under conditions of highly developed productive forces. He said that, under the future communist system, there will be "socialised man, the associated producers, rationally regulating their interchange with Nature, bringing it under their common control, instead of being ruled by it as by the blind forces of Nature; and achieving this with the least expenditure of energy and under conditions most favourable to, and worthy of, their human nature". But this still remains a realm of necessity because "the realm of freedom actually begins only where labour which is determined by necessity and mundane considerations ceases": it lies beyond the sphere of

actual material production. Only beyond the realm of necessity begins the development of human energy which is an end in itself, the true realm of freedom, which, however, can blossom forth only with this realm of necessity as its basis. Here "the shortening of the working day is its basic prerequisite".[18]

We may cite many more examples. But what we have cited show unmistakably the trend of development of the ideas of humanism championed by the founders of Marxism. Their understanding progressed step by step until they arrived at the scientific conclusion regarding the question of the emancipation of man. Ever since Rousseau made the statement that man was born free but everywhere he was in chains, many Western thinkers had been earnestly exploring the way of restoring to man his lost freedom. But they could only grope in the dark. Even such an outstanding philosopher as J. C. Friedrich von Schiller could only entertain illusions which were incapable of being realised. This can best be seen from his *Briefe über die ästhetische Erziehung das Menschen* (*Letters on the Aesthetic Education of Man*). Only Marxism, for the first time in history, has pointed out to mankind the road to freedom. In this sense, we may say that the ideal of humanism can be truly realised only in Marxism.

In view of this, I hold that we cannot diametrically oppose Marxism to humanism in a sweeping manner, much less can we indiscriminately criticise humanism and label it revisionism. We cannot, of course, incorporate Marxism into humanism, for what the former studies is far more than human problems. Nevertheless, Marxism should contain within itself the principles of humanism. Otherwise, Marxism might become its opposite, namely rigid and callous dogmas that do not concern themselves with man at all, or it might even turn itself into a new estranged form of domination over man. Have there not been such lessons in the history of the international communist movement?

III

Humanism is an indispensable element of Marxism. But now there are some comrades who dare not advocate humanism. They always think that the term "humanism" was first used by bourgeois thinkers who also talked most vehemently about it even to the point of using it in their hypocritical preachings to deceive the masses. Consequently, these comrades have concluded that we had better steer clear of humanism. Actually, such a worry is uncalled for. The term "materialism" was also first used by bourgeois philosophers. Should we avoid using it merely on account of this? And should we stop talking about democracy and freedom just because they are what the bourgeoisie talks about most glibly? No, on the contrary. Precisely because the bourgeoisie tries to utilise the banners of humanism, democracy and freedom, we should all the more popularise the correct, Marxist understanding of them so as to expose the limitations and hypocricy of bourgeois humanism, democracy and freedom. We can never remain inactive and let the bourgeoisie do what they like in this respect. We should make people see that humanism, democracy and freedom are not bourgeois monopolies, for the proletariat does far better when it comes to these questions. As long as we stick to the basic Marxist stand, we need not fear that we cannot draw a clear line between us and bourgeois humanism. While it is true that Marxist humanism critically and to a certain extent inherits humanism of the past, there is a basic difference between the two. Especially on a series of major questions, Marxists take a stand which is the opposite of that taken by bourgeois humanists. That is why we can by no means confuse Marxist humanism with the other schools of humanism; we should, instead, regard the former as an advanced, scientific form of humanism.

Marxist humanism has at least the following characteristics that distinguish it from humanism of the other schools.

1. All the other schools of humanism take abstract man, man in general, as their point of departure, and they do not make a concrete, historical analysis of man. In contrast, Marxism affirms the basic fact that, following the disintegration of the primitive commune, social men were divided into different classes, that the existence of these classes is related to specific historical stages of the development of production, and that struggles among different classes constitute the entire written history of human society. All human problems in class society are underlined by this basic fact. There are no supra-class "men in general" besides the countless concrete men who belong to definite classes and carry on their activities in the context of definite class relations. Hence Marxism always insists on looking at, analysing and solving human problems from a class viewpoint. Unlike the other schools of humanism that deny the class character of man, Marxist humanism keeps to the class viewpoint.

2. Although humanists of all the other schools showed their indignation at, and protested against, the various inhuman phenomena existing in society, they fail to recognise their social root and, consequently, the most they can do is to extend sympathy and some assistance to victims; they cannot find a practical way to rid society of such inhuman phenomena for good. Theirs can never be thoroughgoing humanism. On the other hand, Marxism, through penetrating analysis of the various social formations (and the capitalist social structure in particular), pinpoints exploitation of man by man as the most important cause of all the inhuman social phenomena. Marxism scientifically expounds the historical inevitability of the emergence, development

and abolition of the system of exploitation, and makes the abolition of such a system and the ultimate elimination of private ownership the content of its specific programme for struggle. It thus makes the uprooting of all the inhuman phenomena a possibility capable of being realised. In this sense, Marxism is the most thoroughgoing humanism.

3. All humanists other than the Marxist ones are adherents of an idealist conception of history who pin their hope for the building of a future society that embodies the ideas of humanism, on the betterment of "human nature" and the triumph of "eternal justice", or on the emergence of some outstanding individuals and "saviours of mankind". As the theoretical generalisation of the conditions for the emancipation of the proletariat, the most oppressed class in capitalist society, Marxism has replaced all empty talk about "human nature" and "justice" with practical struggles; it has cast away all illusions about there being some "saviours" and affirms, instead, that the genuine emancipation of the masses is a matter for the masses themselves.

4. Unlike some humanists who oppose all force as a matter of principle, Marxists are soberly aware that it is utterly impossible in this world to change everything by virtue of "ravings about love". They hold that the use of revolutionary violence is the most human act when the reactionary classes, to preserve their system which is the most inhuman, use counter-revolutionary violence against the masses. Marxists are, therefore, not bourgeois pacifists, nor are they the Tolstoyan-type advocates of non-violence. They are even more firmly opposed to any indiscriminate use of force, such as treating inhumanely those who have lost the capability of resistance, or "striking someone down to the ground and pinning him there with thousands of the victors' feet".

So much for the main differences between Marxist humanism and humanism of the other schools. As for the entire exact content of the former, it is a subject for separate discussion. Study in China of humanism was completely suspended for many years in the past due to the fact that humanism was always regarded as synonymous with revisionism. Now we must renew this work as a pressing task.

To resume and develop our study of Marxist humanism is not only of theoretical importance but also of great practical significance. Many of the problems we meet in our practical work are related to this. Here are some examples: to some people, the purpose of socialist production is still an open question, even though we have been building socialism for many years. In order that a man may live, there must be a minimum amount of calories and living space — this is a plain truth about which, however, some people were, it seems to me, not quite clear during the previous years. What is worse, some people using the slogan "Fear neither hardships nor death", paid no attention to safety in production and issued arbitrary orders which often meant rash work even at the risk of the workers' very lives. There are other related phenomena such as violating socialist legality, acting in violation of the accepted morality, showing no concern for the welfare of the masses, and taking a laissez-faire attitude to environmental pollution. Ideologically, all of these are directly linked with the disregard of Marxist humanism.

It appears that to properly solve these problems, we must, first and foremost, have a correct understanding of man in socialist society and really treat man as such. With the abolition of the exploiting classes in our socialist society, there should be entirely new relations between men, and consequently Marxist humanism will demonstrate its importance more and more. Socialism should display its superiority over capitalism in all spheres, including the social relations between men which ought to be more in line with humanism. We believe that sooner or later the cold-bloodedness, selfishness, mutual suspicion and deception, and the wolfish relations between men — phenomena characteristic of a capitalist society — will disappear from the globe, to be written down in the annals of human society as a disgrace to mankind.

When all is said and done, the key to the question of recognition of Marxist humanism is emancipation of the mind. We must rid ourselves of the morbid fear of humanism and declare with full justification: Communists are the most thoroughgoing humanists because the purpose of their death-defying struggle is the building of a new world more suitable for mankind to live in, a world where man is really able to develop himself fully, freely and in an all-round way so that he may become man in the true sense of the term and so that the "pre-history" of mankind will be brought to a close. Let the label of "revisionism" be consigned to a museum!

1. Referring to Jiang Qing, Zhang Chunqiao, Yao Wenyuan and Wang Hongwen.
2. "Contribution to the Critique of Hegel's Philosophy of Law", Introduction, Marx and Engels, *Collected Works*, Progress Publishers, Moscow, 1975, Vol. 3. pp.182, 179, 187.
3. *Ibid.*, p.272.
4. *Ibid.*, p.275.
5. *Ibid.*, p.284.
6. *Ibid.*, p.296.
7. *Ibid.*, p.342.
8. *Ibid.*, p.341.
9. *Ibid.*, p.341.
10. *Ludwig Feuerbach and the End of Classical German Philosophy*, Foreign Languages Press, Beijing, 1976, p.38.
11. "Theses on Feuerbach", Marx and Engels, *Collected Works*, Progress Publishers, Moscow, 1976, Vol. 5, p.4.
12. *Ibid.*

13. Marx and Engels, *Collected Works*, Progress Publishers, Moscow, 1975, Vol. 4, pp.36, 37.
14. Marx and Engels, *Collected Works*, Progress Publishers, Moscow, 1976, Vol. 5, p.439.
15. Marx and Engels, *Manifesto of the Communist Party*, FLP, Beijing, 1965, p.58.
16. *Anti-Dühring*, FLP, Beijing, 1976, pp.336, 337.
17. *Ibid.*
18. *Capital*, Foreign Languages Publishing House, Moscow, 1959, Vol. III, pp.799, 800.

IV

Some Questions on the Reassessment of Rosa Luxemburg

Cheng Renqian

Since the close of the Second World War, and since the 1970s in particular, more and more people in many countries have been engaged in the restudy and reassessment of Rosa Luxemburg (1871-1919). From Europe to Asia and to the American continent, and from the developed capitalist countries to the socialist countries and to the Third World, a growing stream of collected and selected works, letters and biographies of Luxemburg as well as treatises on the study of this outstanding proletarian revolutionary and distinguished Marxist theorist have been published. This represents a surge of widespread and sustained interest in Rosa Luxemburg, which has attracted growing attention. The "rediscovery" of this prominent figure over half a century after her death is a special phenomenon in the history of the international communist movement and of Marxism. How should we look at this historical phenomenon? How should we look at and assess Luxemburg in a new light? All this has become a major issue concerning the correct summing-up of the historical experiences (positive as well as negative) of the international communist movement and concerning the development of Marxism in the present era. The author of the present article proposes to make an initial probe into some questions on the reassessment of Luxemburg.

The international background to the renewed interest in Luxemburg and its significance

Marx wrote in *The Eighteenth Brumaire of Louis Bonaparte* more than a century ago: "Thus the awakening of the dead ... served the purpose of glorifying the new struggles, not of parodying the old; of magnifying the given task in the imagination, not of fleeing from its solution in reality; of finding the spirit of revolution once more, not of making its ghost walk about again."[1] This celebrated and meaningful passage from Marx serves as a key to our understanding of the social background and meaning of the "rediscovery" of Luxemburg.

The rise of the interest in Luxemburg is nothing fortuitous: it has its profound social-historical background. On the one hand, it is closely related to the development of contemporary capitalism. On the other, it is organically connected with the evolution of the international communist movement after the Second World War.

Firstly, between the early 1950s and the early 1970s, the developed capitalist countries of the West experienced a high-speed growth in production and the economy as a whole, a growth which was preceded by a scientific and technical revolution. As as a consequence, there was a marked improvement in the material life of the workers, and certain changes in social class structure and the form of ownership system. All this, however, failed to radically change the private ownership of the means of production under capitalism or to eliminate the exploitation of labour by capital. This means that the contradiction inherent in capitalism, i.e., the contradiction between the productive forces and the production relations, remained unresolved. What is more, capitalist development caused not only an unprecedented upswing of the productive forces but also a further progress of science and technology, a progress which aggravated as never before the social malady of capitalism and the form of its modern barbarism. This last aspect can be seen from the following:

— Scientific and technological development multiplied the invention of modern, "scientific" weapons of murder and steadily intensified the arms race, confronting mankind with the threat of a new war.

— The "scientific" and predatory exploitation of the natural resources led to a serious disruption of the ecological balance, threatening the very existence of mankind.

— Scientific and technological advance made possible the tapping of many new material resources, but the enormous newly-added social wealth was concentrated in the hands of a few, increasing the polarisation of the rich and the poor.

— Technical revolution drastically swelled the ranks of the "standing army" of the jobless by reducing the "reserve army" of unemployment, thus worsening the unemployment problem in the capitalist world and causing serious social consequences.

— With scientific and technological advance and rising unemployment, the capitalists forced the workers to increase labour intensity excessively, adding much to the mental and spiritual agony of the workers and causing pernicious psychosis as an evil outcome of the technical revolution.

— Scientific and technological advance changed the structure of the proletariat and expanded its ranks insofar as large numbers of scientific and technical personnel and other non-manual workers were gradually transformed into a component part of the proletariat; all members of the various strata of the proletariat were regarded as different grades of commodities whose prices were subject to market changes and the operation of the law of value, making them enslaved by capital and depriving them of independent personality and human dignity.

— Social groups and religious organisations that were opposed to science and reason mushroomed, and decadence and terrorism were widespread, ruining people spiritually and physically.

The list can be lengthened, but these appalling social phenomena in the developed capitalist countries of the West were already enough to bring people face to face with the harsh reality and make them seriously ponder over the question: since the malignant development of the calamitous crises of capitalism had resulted in mounting modern barbarism, what was the way out for capitalism and what should be done to bring about the revolutionary transformation of capitalist society? People began to seek an answer from the writings of Marx and Rosa Luxemburg, a pioneer in the study of modern capitalism. It is against such a background that people made an active probe into the famous and thought-provoking thesis raised by Luxemburg as far back as half a century ago: socialism, or degeneration into barbarism?[2] Many Luxemburg scholars hold that, despite the new situation and the new problems of contemporary capitalism, this incisive and point-blank thesis of Luxemburg's retains its powerful vitality, and that it manifests great theoretical and practical significance so that it remains the most important problem facing contemporary capitalism. This shows that, although Luxemburg did not live to see the actual development of contemporary capitalism, she foresaw and expounded what is in store for it by virtue of her penetrating insight and far-sightedness as a Marxist theorist, and clearly and unerringly pointed out to the people the historical challenge they face as well as the goal of their struggle: socialism is the only alternative to the sinking of modern capitalism into barbarism; socialism is a historical necessity. It is acknowledged that the series of Luxemburg's original theses on the waging of the socialist revolution in the developed capitalist countries is enlightening. This has prompted people to combine the study of Luxemburg's theories with the study of contemporary society so as to explore from the theoretical angle the prospects of eradicating modern capitalist barbarism and realising the objective of socialism.

Meanwhile, as far as revolutionary practice is concerned, the 1960s and the 1970s were a period of worldwide turbulence and wave-like revolutionary struggles. Europe, heartland of the developed capitalist countries, witnessed a world-shaking mass struggle of strike in France in 1968, followed by large-scale mass movements in Italy, Portugal and Spain. The year 1974 is remembered for the economic crisis in the whole capitalist world that was the most serious in post-war years and had major social consequences. It fanned the workers' smouldering discontent at current social reality and their stern criticism of the capitalist system; at the same time, it aroused an interest in a reappraisal and restudy of the questions of mass strike struggle and of the revolutionary crisis which Luxemburg had systematically expounded. It is generally admitted that the relevant theses of Luxemburg's are highly evocative and of great practical significance and, therefore, helpful in raising the level of the current struggle of the working class. Besides, there are those in Western Germany and some other Western countries who, in their longing for a change in reality, make use of Luxemburg's views in lashing at re-emerging Bernsteinism, opposing social reformism, and striving to bring the resurgent working-class movement in Western Europe into the revolutionary, Marxist orbit and explore the path of achieving socialism through revolutionary struggles.

It can be seen that the "rediscovered" thinking and theories of Rosa Luxemburg have become a powerful ideological weapon of people in the developed capitalist countries of today, a powerful weapon which helps them to arrive at a correct understanding of reality, stimulates the revolutionary spirit of the working class, and encourages them in their effort to fight against the exsisting social order and seek the path of accomplishing socialism. Her thinking and theories have thus taken on a new lease of life and a new meaning. We can draw the conclusion that the development of contemporary capitalism and the problems besetting it, as well as the exploration of the way of bringing about the transformation of capitalist society, constitute part of the mighty impetus to the wave of interest in Luxemburg.

Secondly, the post-war development of the international communist movement and the changes it has undergone also help to push Rosa Luxemburg to the foreground of history. As early as the end of the 1940s, the appearence of the "Yugoslav question" gave rise to a deep interest among people in the different modes of socialism. The triumph of the Chinese revolution in 1949 and the subsequent successes in China's socialist construction have drawn the close attention of people in the question of how Marxism is to be combined with the revolutionary practice in a given country. The death of Stalin in 1953 and the criticism of the personality cults that followed, the rise of Khrushchevism and the subsequent evolution of the Soviet Union, and the Poznan and Hungarian incidents of 1956, all induced people to make a many-sided probe into the various questions concerning Marxism-Leninism and socialism. Particular mention should be made of the events that transpired at the turn of the 1960s-1970s, such as Czechoslovakia's reform movement in 1968 which was followed by Soviet invasion of that country, and the the Polish incidents in 1968-70. All these events not only exposed the true features of Soviet hegemonism, but also laid bare the disadvantages of some East European countries copying the "Soviet Model" as well as the glaring failings in their system, thus again making the questions of structural reform and socialist democracy major issues riveting the attention of people and causing controversies among them. It is in the context of the new circumstances and new problems facing the international communist movement, and in the process of exploring the model of socialism and debating the questions of democracy and reform, that Luxemburg's theories on socialism — especially her uniquely creative views on the relationship between the dictatorship of the proletariat and socialist democracy — were discovered. Her theories and views are so helpful that many Luxemburg scholars have come to regard her as one of the pioneers of modern socialism. They are of the opinion that Luxemburg's views on the necessity of relying on the masses of the people and of bringing into full play their historical initiative and creativeness in the fight for socialism; her exposition of socialist democracy; and her thesis that, following the proletariat's seizure of power, extension of democracy is an effective guarantee against bureaucracy, arbitrary individual rule and the degeneration of the revolution — all these views of Luxemburg's are scientifically grounded foresights whose correctness has repeatedly been borne out by the historical experience of the international communist movement. They have, therefore, become an asset of this movement.

It is thus clear that the development of, and the changes in, the present-day international communist movement, the drawbacks in and reform of the system of some East European countries, and the deep-set and worldwide development of the theory and practice of socialism, combine to furnish another part of the great impetus to the rising interest in Luxemburg.

What has been described above enables us to draw this basic conclusion: the increasing worldwide interest in Luxemburg is by no means confined to assessing her merits and demerits or her historical role, for it has a much deeper and more far-reaching social root. Luxemburg's thinking and theories are still of profound theoretical as well as practical significance for the era we live in. Herein lies the basic reason for the "rediscovery" of Luxemburg in the 1970s and for the mounting interest in and earnest study of her theories. To restudy and reassess Luxemburg is the duty of the struggle for socialism in the developed capitalist countries, the duty of the building of socialism in the socialist countries, the duty of the development of Marxism, and the duty of the time.

How should we understand the differences between Luxemburg and Lenin?

How should we look at the differences between Luxemburg and Lenin on a number of questions and how should we look at the consequent controversies between them — this has always been at the heart of the debate on the assessment of Luxemburg, and one of the key questions involved in our current reassessment of her.

For nearly 20 years Luxemburg and Lenin maintained a relation of friendship and co-operation. During the early years of the 20th century when crises and wars interwove with one another, Luxemburg and Lenin coordinated their efforts in opposing opportunism and imperialism. There were, of course, recurring differences in viewpoints between them, which led to controversies. The first open polemic occurred in 1904 over the organisational principles of the Russian Bolshevik Party, namely, over the question of the relationship between democracy and centralism. The year 1908 saw the second major difference between Luxemburg and Lenin, this time on the question of national self-determination, a difference which precipitated a controversy that was to last many years. More divergent views and controversies appeared in later years, over the relationship between Bolshevism ann Menshevism and over the theory of capital accumulation. While in prison, Luxemburg warmly hailed and appraised highly the Russian October Socialist Revolution which proceeded and triumphed under Lenin's leadership. She held that the proletarian revolution that first won victory was of tremendous significance as a turing point in world history. She also fully affirmed the necessity of the dictatorship of the proletariat.

It is, however, also while she was imprisoned, namely, in 1918, that Luxemburg wrote an important and yet unfinished article entitled "The Russian Revolution". Never published in her life-time, the manuscript of this article sharply criticised some policies being carried out then by Lenin and the Bolshevik Party. In 1922, Paul Levi, who had by then left the German Communist Party, obtained a duplicate of the manuscript of "The Russian Revolution" and made it public. In his preface to it, which was even longer than the article itself, Levi distorted Luxemburg's original meaning in an attempt to conceal his own attack on Lenin and the Bolshevik Party. This resulted in a heated polemic in the international communist movement of the time. Thenceforth, the article "The Russian Revolution" became a focal point of controversy in the assessment of Luxemburg, and this controversy has been going on right to the present day.

These examples show that there really existed some differences between Luxemburg and Lenin on a number of questions, and that in certain cases they vastly differed from each other. But how should we understand these differences?

First and foremost, it is essential to ascertain the nature of the differences between Luxemburg and Lenin. It should be pointed out that both Luxemburg and Lenin were great proletarian revolutionaries living in the same era, that both of them upheld the basic principles of Marxism, and that under the new circumstances when history had entered the era of imperialism they both strove to develop Marxism continuously and to push the proletarian revolution movement to a new height. So far as a series of basic questions of Marxism is concerned, for instance, the theory of class struggle and the theory of the state and especially the principal aspects of the questions of the proletarian revolution and the dictatorship of the proletariat, Luxemburg and Lenin had indentical or basically identical views. Nevertheless, they held divergent and even widely divergent views as regards some concrete methods and tactics for realising the revolutionaary tasks, for instance, the peasant question, the national question and the question of democracy. This means that their differences were not diametrical conflicts of view derived from different attitudes to the basic principles of Marxism. That is why we cannot exaggerate their differences one-sidedly or by treating them in isolation from the other related questions, much less can we artificially set Luxemburg against Lenin. We should see that identity of views was primary and fundamental while divergence of views was secondary, not fundamental. We must on no account obscure the demarcation line between the two aspects if we are to correctly analyse the nature of the question under discussion and correctly assess Luxemburg.

Secondly, we should analyse the root cause of the differences between Luxemburg and Lenin. The fundamental reason why Luxemburg differed from Lenin on certain questions was that they made theoretical exploration and were engaged in revolutionary practice in different socio-political conditions, and that they acquired different subjective recognition of different objective conditions in which they lived. They were contemporaries living in a period of transition from the proletariat accumulating strength to its launching direct revolutionary onslaughts. This is the common point Luxemburg and Lenin shared with each other. Since the conditions in Germany were markedly different from those in Russia, however, they had to conduct revolutionary activities under totally different circumstances, which meant that the revolutionary tactics and methods they employed were necessarily different in this or that respect. Proceeding from the actual situation characterised by absolute tsarist Russian autocracy and sluggish capitalist development, Lenin creatively applied the basic principles of Marx and combined Marxism with the practice of the Russian revolution, thereby developing Marxism and advancing it to the plane of Leninism and guiding the Russian revolution on to the path of victory. On the other hand, carrying out revolutionary activities in a developed capitalist country, that is, in Germany where parliamentary democracy was more sophisticated, Luxemburg could not but take into account the objective reality there and assume some characteristics of her own in seeking the way of applying the basic principles of Marxism to the revolutionary practice in her own country. She could not but have some views different for Lenin's on certain questions of tactics. Nonetheless, she contributed enormously to the enrichment and development of Marxism. We must, of course, note that, conditioned as she was by the environment of peaceful capitalist development and of chiefly open and legal working-class struggles, and surrounded and influenced as she was by the sweeping opportunism of the Second International, Luxemburg suffered from a certain lack of thoroughness and clarity and even made certain mistakes in her theoretical presentation on some questions. Precisely because of this, she often based herself on the German situation in her controversies with Lenin, during which she insisted on her own views; she did not observe and analyse things in the context of reality obtaining in Russia and thus some of her criticisms of Lenin were at variance with facts, one-sided and even incorrect. We should, therefore, use the analytical, i.e., dialectical, method in exploring the cause of the differences between Luxemburg and Lenin. Only thus can we differentiate in a truth-seeking way what is right from what is erroneous in Luxemburg's theoretical expositions and so arrive at sound conclusions.

Let us cite some examples to illustrate our point. Although on the question of the organisational principles of the Party Luxemburg and Lenin agreed with each other that there should be a centralised and unified party, they differed on the exact nature and degree of centralism. To put it in a nutshell, Luxemburg stressed more democracy while Lenin was more concerned with centralism. This is readily understandable if one bears in mind the different social conditions of Russia and Germany. As Russia was under absolute autocracy and the workers' movement there was weak and subjected to cold-blooded repression, Lenin emphasised a high degree of centralism, the role of a small number of professional revolutionaries and the necessity and importance of secret work. This was fully in accord with the requirements of the struggle of the time. The situation was different in Germany where the proletarian party which had a legal status could conduct its work openly and its organisations at various levels could elect delegates for congresses which were held regularly, and the Party had its own newspapers and journals and enjoyed a certain measure of freedom of speech and activity. Consequently and understandably, Luxemburg stressed inner-Party democracy. It is, nevertheless, obviously impracticable and hence wrong to demand that the Russian party act in the same manner despite the different situation it was in. But does it follow that Luxemburg was totally wrong in her argument with Lenin on the question of the organisational principles of the Party? It does not. It was exactly in such argument that she not only laid stress on the development of inner-Party democracy, which is correct from the long-term point of view, but also pioneered the initial concept of "social-democratic centralism", i.e., democratic centralism. She pointed out that social-democratic centralism is nothing but the absolute centralisation of the will of the politically conscious vanguard of the working class which is engaged in struggle; and that it is the "self-centralism" of the leading stratum of the proletariat, the rule of the overwhelming majority within the party organisation of the proletariat itself.[3] Luxemburg also said that such centralism must rest on the basis of democracy, and that there can only be the subordination of the individual members to the organisation and the subordination of the minority to the majority. She emphasised that power must not be overconcentrated, still less should it be concentrated in the hands of a few leaders, for otherwise it will help the growth of arbitrary individual rule and drain the vitality of the Party organisation. Despite that Lenin at the time did not follow Luxemburg's advice, he formally recognised "the principle of democratic centralism" at the Fourth (Unity) Congress of the Russian Social-Democratic Labour Party held in 1906,[4] and later had it incorporated into the Party constitution. He did so in keeping with the development of the revolutionary situation and the changes in the overall conditions following the Russian revolution of 1905. This shows cleary that Lenin was influenced to a certain extent by Luxemburg. The preliminary presentation of the concept of democratic centralism is one of Luxemburg's contributions to the Marxist theory of Party-building.

Another example is that, in the manuscript of her article "The Russian Revolution", Luxemburg sharply criticised some policies adopted by the Soviet government shortly after the October Revolution. Facts showed that her criticisms were ungrounded, one-sided and inappropriate on many points. The reason is likewise that Luxemburg was not familiar with the specific situation of the Russian revolution, and that she underestimated the complexity of the class struggle confronting it. We should, however, look at the question also from another angle: precisely because the imprisoned Luxemburg did not take part in the October Revolution she was not limited by the situation then existing in Russia. As the saying goes, "An onlooker sees things more clearly than those involved." So Luxemburg could analyse and deal with the experiences of the October Revolution scientifically and in a historical perspective. She pointed out that the October Revolution was a socialist revolution waged under abnormal and extremely difficult conditions when the First World War was still going on. Consequently, what the Russian revolution had done cannot be the "peak of perfection", and there should be no uncritical praise or blind copying of it; only with well-thought analysis and criticism can it be possible to discover the treasurehouse of its experiences and lessons. That is why Luxemburg maintained that on no account should one regard the experiences of the October Revolution in absolute terms, much less should one theoretically make formulas of each and every part of the tactics the Bolshevik Party was compelled to adopt under abnormal conditions, and then recommend the whole to the international proletariat as a flawless model of socialist tactics. She warned that this is something dangerous, for it means disservice to international socialism.[5] History has borne out that this attitude of Luxemburg's is scientific, and that hers are far-sighted and sagacious views. She proved to be the first (except Lenin) in the history of the international communist movement to sum up the historical experiences of the October Revolution by using the Marxist dialectical viewpoint. Here we find one of her major historical contributions. As a matter of fact, Lenin himself examined the October Revolution in the same way. While enunciating the international significance of certain fundamental features of the October Revolution, he opposed regarding its experiences in an absolute manner. He pointed out that "certain fundamental features of our revolution have a significance which is not local, not peculiarly national, not Russian only, but international ... Of course, it would be a very great mistake to exaggerate this truth and to apply it not only to certain fundamental features of our revolution."[6] What is regrettable is that, after the death of Luxemburg and Lenin, some people have forgotten their exhortation and institutionalised, canonised and dogmatised everything Soviet, gradually made the Soviet experience a rigid, fossilised and bureaucratised model and tried to push it everywhere for others to copy mechanically. Everybody is clear about the serious consequences of all of this.

Our analysis of these two examples tells that what is essential regarding the differences between Luxemburg and Lenin is to trace their social root and to make the dialectical approach of "one divides into two" instead of totally negating or obliterating the views of either side. Even on certain questions over which Luxemburg and Lenin had heated controversies, their views were mutually complementary instead of being mutually antithetical. Far from being heresies, some of Luxemburg's theoretical views are scientifically original.

Thirdly, practice must be taken as the criterion for judging right and wrong. Practice is the sole criterion for verifying a truth and the only reliable yardstick for assessing historical figures. In the past, Luxemburg's mistakes were exaggerated and criticised in absolute terms and her theoretical contributions were minimised and even written off because, fundamentally speaking, there was no scientific standard of appraisal and verdicts were passed merely in accordance with certain theses advanced by some revolutionary leaders, especially Stalin. *Rosa Luxemburg: a Brief Critical Biography* written by Fred Oelssner and published in East Germany during the early 1950s bases itself on some isolated quotations from Stalin and brushes aside the whole of Luxemburg's theory as "an erroneous system". It criticises as erroneous all her views which are different from Lenin's. Although, generally speaking, *Rosa Luxemburg: a Brief Biography* written by R. Y. Evzerov in collaboration with I. S. Yazhborovskaya and published in the Soviet Union during the 1970s and *Rosa Luxemburg: Her Role in the German Workers' Movement* co-authored by A. Laschitzy and G. Radczun and published in East Germany also in the 1970s — although both works make a relatively objective assessment of Luxemburg, they stick to the wrong viewpoint that everything said by Lenin is truth whenever they touch on the differences between Luxemburg and Lenin. They either describe as erroneous Luxemburg's views which are different from Lenin's or, in an oversimplified manner, say that her thinking "failed to reach the height of Lenin's" even though it is not totally reproachable. Both books overlook or refuse to admit that there are in Luxemburg's thinking and theories many creative and penetrating views that retain their tremendous theoretical value and practical significance up to the present. Now, in order to correctly assess Luxemburg, we must discard such an unscientific method which runs counter to the principles of historical materialism, and make pratice (historical practice of the time and in the subsequent years) as the criterion for testing the worth of some of Luxemburg's ideas and theories. For example, when expounding the theory of democracy, she made criticisms of Lenin and the Bolshevik Party, criticisms which contained mistakes if judged in the context of the actual situation confronting the Russian revolution in those years. But she did foresee the evil consequences that can possibly arise from the undesirable practice growing within the ranks of the revolutionary movement, i.e., overconcentration of power and lack of democracy. Her criticisms were, therefore, not so much an utopian and over-critical effort as an attempt at exploring in practice and expounding in theory the way of achieving a high level of genuine democracy. Judged from a long-term point of view (i.e., in terms of the prospects of historical development), considering the historical stage of the dictatorship of the proletariat as a whole, and bearing in mind the historical experiences and lessons of the dictatorship of the proletariat in the previous half a century or more, we can say that Luxemburg acted like a trail blazer in the international communist movement and contributed to the development of Marxism when she raised inner-Party democracy and people's democracy to such a high plane, regarding them as the basis and prerequisite of the sound development of the Party and of the proper exercise of the dictatorship of the proletariat, as the air and sunshine so vital to both, and as something the Party and the proletarian state cannot do without even for a moment. This much has been fully and repeatedly proved by the rich practice of the international communist movement.

How might we correctly assess Luxemburg's theory of democracy?

As stated previously, Luxemburg's theory of democracy — inner-Party democracy and people's democracy — is the most significant and most valuable part of her ideological and theoretical legacy as well as one of the most heatedly debated and most divergent questions among Luxemburg scholars for over half a century. Many Western scholars think highly of Luxemburg's thesis on democracy, setting her up as the initiator of "democratic socialism" or of communism of the "democratic type". Scholars in the Soviet Union and some East European countries, however, have mostly changed from an attitude of total negation of Luxemburg's theory of democracy to one of sidestepping or keeping silent on the question, for they fear discussion of the crucial questions related to the "Soviet Model" as much as they fear fire. So, in general, far from reaching a consensus, Luxemburg scholars of the various countries take two altogether different stands. How, then, should we correctly assess this theory of democracy, especially of the relationship between democracy and centralism and that between democracy and dictatorship — a question which, despite scores of years of controversy within the international communist movement, has yet to be solved satisfactorily?

The author of the present article deems that the "Resolution on Certain Questions in the History of Our Party Since the Founding of the People's Republic of China" adopted in June 1981 by the Sixth Plenary Session of the Eleventh Central Committee of the

Chinese Communist Party furnishes a valuable key to the correct summing up of the historical experiences of the Chinese Communist Party and to the proper solution, in theory as well as in practice, of the question of democracy. It is also of great reference value for the correct summing up of the historical experiences of the international communist movement and for the proper appraisal of Luxemburg's theory of democracy.

Luxemburg's theory of inner-Party democracy may be roughly summarised as follows:

1. *The correct handling of the relationship between democracy and centralism.* The essence of this question is, in the final analysis, the relationship between the masses and the leadership. Luxemburg said emphatically that centralism must be built on the basis of democracy because, otherwise, it will be "isolated and exclusive". This means that centralism within the Party organisation must rest on the basis of democracy characterised by direct reliance on the masses, that is, on their pioneering spirit. Luxemburg held that there must in no way be an insurmountable wall between the masses and the leading core composed of Party cadres chosen for long-term leadership work. She, therefore, stessed that measures must be taken to develop inner-Party demcracy, turn to good account the initiative and creativeness of the Party members and the non-Party people and strengthen the Party member's democratic supervision of the leading organs of the Party.

2. *The relationship between the central and local authorities.* On this question, Luxemburg stressed that there should not be excessive concentration of power. She maintained that, since the struggle for socialism is the cause of the whole class and the whole Party, it is obvious that Party organisations at the various levels must enjoy freedom of action so as independently to make use of all the means available under the circumstances prevailing and strengthen the struggle

and develop the revolutionary pioneering spirit.[8] Party centralism should not be built on the basis of the blind obedience and mechanical subordination of the Party organisations at the various levels and the masses of the Party members to the central organs, nor should their be blind subordination of all Party organisations to the central bodies in all their activities including the minute details thereof.[9] To put it briefly, Luxemburg held that, under centralised guidance, local Party organisations at various levels should enjoy the necessary power devolved on them and certain power of decision. She also pointed out that only with the development of inner-Party democracy, free discussion of the major and overall issues and freedom of criticism can there be perfect coordination and solidarity and unity of the Party organisations from the central down to the local levels, or can there be healthy development of the Party as a whole. Otherwise, bureaucracy, privileges and autocracy will be in vogue within the Party, and the Party may even degenerate.

3. *The relationship between the leaders and the Party.* In line with her consistent thinking on the development of inner-Party democracy, Luxemburg put forward some incisive views on this weighty question. She held that the Party should have outstanding leaders of its own, that leaders should embody the will of the whole Party and that, on the premise that there is rule of the overwhelming majority in the Party, its outstanding leaders should clearly understand and fully develop the objective role of their own among the masses, ensure the subordination of the local interests to the overall interests of the Party as a whole, and make the masses aware of the objective law of historical development and thus guide them in fulfilling the mission entrusted by history. The proletariat's struggle for socialism is like a chorus in action, and the leaders should act as the "spokesmen", i.e., as the embodiment of the will of the

masses.[10] Leaders of the Party must abide by its discipline, which can only mean subordination to the will and ideas of the overwhelming majority. No Party leaders can stand above the Party organisation of the general Party membership, still less can they blindly consider themselves heroes capable of making history. This is because, as the conscious adherent and intellectual product of historical materialism, the Social-Democratic Party does not recognise any cult of the heroes, and also because the more unequivocally and consciously the leaders of such a party make themselves the spokesmen of the will and aspirations of the politically conscious and embattled masses and make themselves the embodiment of the objective law of the working-class movement — the more they do so, the greater will their capacity and prestige become.[11]

The above description indicates that, despite some inappropriate criticisms Luxemburg levelled at Lenin in her debate with him on the organisational principles of the Party, she did set forth many brilliant and thought-provoking views on inner-Party democracy, which are a contribution to the Marxist theory of Party-building. Democratic centralism is the organisational principle of a Marxist party. By and large, the problems which cropped up within the Party over the years were due not to the system of democratic centralism itself but to its disruption. Meanwhile, we should see that overconcentration of power and lack of democracy were also among the major causes of the various defects that appeared under new historical conditions. Adversely affecting the role of collective wisdom, the above defects were chiefly responsible for the situation within the Party where "what I say goes" and for the patriarchal rule, bureaucracy, personal arbitrariness, individuals standing above the Party organisation, and the personality cult, all of which were prevalent for a time. In our reassessment of Luxemburg today, we should, therefore, duly affirm her theoretical contribution to inner-Party democracy and draw the necessary lesson and, under the new historical conditions, gradually set up and perfect our Party's leadership system marked by a high degree of democracy.

Now let us briefly describe Luxemburg's theory of people's democracy, namely, socialist democracy or democracy within the framework of the state system.

1. Dictatorship of the proletariat is democracy in a socialist sense. In her works on the Russian revolution and the German revolution, Luxemburg all along regarded the dictatorship of the proletariat as synonymous with socialist democracy, a taking the two as different presentations of one and the same concept. She wrote that the task of the proletariat is to create, following the conquest of power, socialist democracy in place of bourgeois democracy, and that socialist democracy is nothing but the dictatorship of the proletariat.[12] She pointed out specifically that democracy and dictatorship are a dialectical unity; and that to realise socialism it is necessary both to ensure democracy and repress the resistance of reaction even though the use of force should be limited and dictatorship exercised only over the enemy who is in the minority. Her conclusion is: without democracy, there will be no dictatorship, no socialism.

2. Socialist democracy is democracy for the masses, for the majority. Luxemburg held that socialist democracy, i.e., the dictatorship of the proletariat, requires the leadership of the Party. But such dictatorship must be the cause of the class as a whole, instead of a cause carried out by a minority of leaders in the name of the class. That is to say, the dictatorship of the proletariat must, in its every step, rely on the enthusiastic participation of the masses, place itself under their direct influence and accept public supervision.[13] It is imperative to realise socialism and

expropriate the capitalist class in conformity with the will and wishes of the protetariat as the majority, i.e., with the spirit of socialist democracy. Without the conscious will and action of the proletariat that is in the majority, there will be no socialism.[14] Luxemburg further pointed out that there is no enthusiasm on the part of the masses in the absence of socialist democracy, direct mass participation and public supervision; and that, consequently, the nation's political life will be stifled, leading to the widespread phenomena of some people enjoying privileges and of bureaucracy and autocracy and to the steady sapping of the vitality of the socialist system and even to the danger of the state sliding towards totalitarianism.

Moreover, proceeding from the thesis that democracy means democracy for the majority, Luxemburg dwelt on the relationship between inner-Party democracy and people's democracy. For over half a century, people have held widely divergent views regarding the following famous passage from Luxemburg over which there has been unending controversy: if freedom is given only to supporters of the government, only to members of a specific party, then it is no freedom, whatever the size of that party. Freedom is always freedom of having those different views. This is not due to "righteous" fanaticism, for the whole educative, beneficial and purifying role of political freedom is connected with this essential aspect. The role of freedom disappears as soon as it is turned into privilege.[15] There are some who contend that here Luxemburg was advocating "great democracy" and anarchism and calling for the extension of democracy to dissidents who oppose the socialist system. The author of the present article thinks that this is a misunderstanding. Judged from the whole context and meaning of the above passage, Luxemburg was stressing the extensive character and importance of people's democracy.

Readers are invited to discuss whether the following understanding of the passage is more precise. What Luxemburg was driving at is that it is essential for the dictatorship of the proletariat not only to develop inner-Party democracy and extend democratic rights to the Party members but also develop people's democracy and extend maximum democratic rights and political freedom to the masses of the people so as to give full reins to the enthusiasm of both the Party members and the non-Party people and put the socialist system on a broader and more solid mass basis. Luxemburg held that this is the only effective means to forestall corruption, privileges, personal arbitrariness and bureaucracy and to give scope to the aforesaid "purifying" role. She understood that there will unavoidably be different and even erroneous ideas among the masses; that, on the premise of upholding socialism, all should be free to express all kinds of different opinions and the different opinions of the minority should be tolerated and given due consideration; and that all should have their say instead of acting only at the dictates of a certain individual. In the meantime, Luxemburg repeatedly emphasised that the level of political understanding and consciousness of the masses should be raised through better political-ideological education and training. As she saw it, this is an important factor and prerequisite for practicing people's democracy. In this sense, Luxemburg's views concerning the question under discussion are sound and far-sighted. At the same time however, it must be pointed out that Luxemburg's formulation of political democracy and freedom is imperfect, not precise enough in that she did not, from the political angle, give a precise exposition or define the category of the question of having different views among the people. This is theoretically a defect which may, in practice, make people confuse the concept of having different views with the concept of being a dissident. Besides, on more than one occasion she called for "unrestricted" democracy and freedom, and this is obviously imprecise in theory and unworkable in practice. On the other hand, it must be added that we cannot be too exacting with Luxemburg's theoretical shortcoming under review because it is contained only in a marginal note on a manuscript yet to be finalised. In short, for all its failings, Luxemburg's thesis that a socialist democracy is democracy for the masses of the people as the majority shines with intellectual brilliance even to this day.

3. Socialist democracy includes democracy in political, social and economic life, and it requires the correct handling of the relationship between power and responsibility and between freedom and discipline. Apart from enhancing the political understanding of the masses through political-ideological education, there must be legal means to ensure genuine socialist democracy. With concise and yet powerful language, Luxemburg pointed out that the essence of socialist society lies in that the broad masses of the workers are no longer the ruled but have become masters of the whole of their own political and economic life, and in that the proletarian masses must become consciously thinking and decision-making masters of the production process instead of remaining soulless and passive tools in the hands of the capitalists. They must foster in themselves a sense of responsibility befitting the active members of society and the only masters of social wealth. They must work enthusiastically without the watchful eyes of the capitalist-type overseers, accomplish the highest labour productivity without compulsion, observe discipline without being fettered, and maintain order without the threat of whips. Dedicating themselves to the good of society as a whole, they should have the loftiest ideal, observe the strictest discipline and display a true sense of responsibility of

citizens.[16] Luxemburg also wrote that socialism is an economic, social and legal system, and that the socialist democratic system should be guranteed by socialist legality. This is because, according to Luxemburg, legality in each and every era is but a product of the revolution; if it can be said that revolution is a creative political act in the history of a given class, legislation is its continuation in the political sphere.[17]

It it thus evident that Luxemburg was an ardent champion and energetic expounder of people's democracy, i.e., socialist democracy, and that she made her unique contribution to the development of the theory of socialism, and the theory of democracy in particular. Her theory of democracy is rich in enlightening interpretation of the question of masses — class — party — leaders. Due to her early death, however, this theory of hers remains incomplete and partly imprecise and inappropriate. We must take the approach of "one divides into two" and make a scientific and truth-seeking analysis and exploration of it in order to discover its real worth, which will be of great reference value for the advance of the Marxist theory of democracy under new historical conditions. It is totally wrong for some Soviet and East German scholars to negate and write off Luxemburg's theory of democracy as heresy. On the other hand, it is also wrong for some Western scholars to look upon Luxemburg as the initiator of "democratic socialism". It must be stated emphatically that there exists a clear demarcation line between the socialist democracy championed by Luxemburg on the one hand and the "democratic socialism" pushed by the opportunists on the other. The "democratic socialism" acclaimed by the opportunists means divorce from the basic principles of Marxism and renunciation of the comprehensive theory of the development of capitalism; interpreting "democracy" as the only means and road, it denies the necessity of relying on the revolutionary potential of the proletariat for the realisation of socialism and advertises the reformist and peaceful road instead. In contrast, Luxemburg took the principled stand of revolutionary Marxism and stressed the necessity of believing in and relying on the proletariat's revolutionary potential and history-making initiative, and stressed the realisation of socialism through proletarian dictatorship, i.e., socialist democracy. By no means can this be mentioned in the same breath with the so-called "democratic socialism". Moreover, in the 1970s, the new historical conditions of capitalist development gave rise to the ideological trend and movement of what is known as "Eurocommunism" in the developed European capitalist countries. Eurocommunism stands for exploring the road of realising socialism by proceeding from the particular conditions of capitalism in Europe. Dismissing any existing "model" and disapproving the reformist road of "democratic socialism" declared by the European Social-Democratic parties, it calls for participation in government through democratic means and then the step-by-step advance to the objective of socialism. It is against this historical background that some Luxemburg scholars in Europe and America and theorists of Eurocommunism regard Luxemburg as the ideological forerunner of Eurocommunism. The author of the present article thinks that this view is debatable. It takes in-depth study to determine whether in some respects there are any internal relations between Luxemburg's theory of democracy and Eurocommunism.

 The above exposition leads to the conclusion that Luxemburg's theory of democracy has made indelible contribution to the enrichment and development of Marxism, and that it has been exercising a tremendous influence on the present era. Consequently, we cannot but pay close attention to and make a special study of it in our effort to reassess Luxemburg.

* * *

History is advancing, and the revolution is forging ahead. In the new situation of present-day capitalist development together with its new problems and in the circumstances where both the theory and practice of socialism are developing steadily and penetratingly, the "rediscovery" and reassessment of Luxemburg's thinking and theories are of considerable benefit to our study and development of Marxism in a new historical context and to our building of a powerful socialist China with a high level of democracy and culture.

1. Marx, *The Eighteenth Brumaire of Louis Bonaparte*, Foreign Languages Press, Beijing, 1978, p.11.
2. *Cf. Collected Works of Rosa Luxemburg*, German edition, Vol. 4, p.496.
3. *Cf. Collected Works of Rosa Luxemburg*, German edition, Vol. 1, Part 2, p.429.
4. *Cf.* Lenin, *Collected Works*, Foreign Languages Publishing House, Moscow, 1962, Vol. 10, p.163.
5. *Cf. Collected Works of Rosa Luxemburg*, German edition, Vol. 4, pp.463-64.
6. *"Left-Wing" Communism, an Infantile Disorder*, FLP, Beijing, 1975, pp.1-2.
7. *Resolution on CPC History (1949-81)*, FLP, 1981, p.79.
8. *Cf. Collected Works of Rosa Luxemburg*, German edition, Vol. 1, Part 1, p.438.
9. *Cf. ibid.*, p.429.
10. *Cf. Selected Works of Rosa Luxemburg*, Warsaw edition, 1959, Vol. 1, p.588.
11. *Cf. Collected Works of Rosa Luxemburg*, German edition, Berlin, 1972, Vol. 2, p.280.
12. *Cf.* Kohanski, *Rosa Luxemburg*, Warsaw edition, 1976, pp.390-91.
13. *Cf.* Luxemburg, *The Russian Revolution*, German edition, Vol. 2, p.435.
14. *Cf. Selected Works of Rosa Luxemburg*, Vol. 2, p.435.
15. *Cf. The Russian Revolution*, German edition, Berlin, 1922, p.109.
16. *Cf.* Kohanski, *Rosa Luxemburg*, Warsaw edition, 1976, pp.390-91.
17. *Cf. The Russian Revolution*, German edition, Berlin, 1922.

The Contributors

Su Shaozhi is a Fellow of the Chinese Academy of Social Sciences, a member of its Academic Committee, Director of its Institute of Marxism-Leninism and Mao Zedong Thought, and Professor of Economics at Beijing University.

Wu Dakun is Professor in the Department of Political Economy, China People's University, Beijing.

Ru Xin is the Vice-President of the Chinese Academy of Social Sciences.

Cheng Renqian is Vice-President of Shanxi University.

The papers are translated by **Zhao Shuhan**.

Democracy and Socialism in China

Su Shaozhi in discussion with Michael Barratt Brown, Wlodzimierz Brus, John Eaton and Andras Hegedus

What is happening in China today?
Few people in Europe are aware of the extent of the discussion which concerned the Chinese leaders and Communist Party activists during the convulsive readjustments which have taken place since the death of Mao. In this little book Su Shaozhi, the influential spokesman of the Institute of Marxism-Leninism-Mao Zedong Thought, exchanges opinions with some distinguished European socialist economists. Su Shaozhi's considered views on the huge questions and choices presented by China's development, and by her recent changes in political direction are carefully questioned by Michael Barratt Brown, Wlodzimierz Brus, John Eaton and Andras Hegedus.
For the first time in recent years, this discussion brings together independent East European specialists, Western scholars, and an official spokesman of the Chinese point of view.
These papers have also been published in China.

ISBN 0 85124 343 6
Price £1.95

Bertrand Russell House, Gamble Street, Nottingham, UK.
Tel. (0602) 708318.

SPOKESMAN

N.I. BUKHARIN
Selected Writings on the State and the Transition to Socialism
Edited by Richard B. Day

For the first time in English, the key writings of **N.I. BUKHARIN** during the tumultuous years from 1915 to 1929 are made available. This compelling selection prepared by Professor Day reflects the suppressed half of the central debate preoccupying Soviet economists and Party leaders in the first decade after the Revolution.

At issue was the establishment of socialist production relations in a country struggling with an extraordinarily burdensome history. Emerging from centuries of tsarist tyranny, the country was ravaged for years together by the First World War, the Revolution itself and the period of War Communism. It then began a convulsive series of experiments; trade liberalisation through the New Economic Policy (NEP), which in turn gave way to preparations for the first Five Year Plan. This phase joined with the turmoil of the forced collectivisation of agriculture.

As one of the leading theorists of the Communist Party, during the twenties Bukharin joined issue with Trotsky in sharp debate over the preferred course and rate of Soviet industrialisation. In the political struggle of these epoch-making years, Bukharin and his ideas were ultimately outlawed by Stalin.

The selection includes:

Towards a Theory of the Imperialist State (1915)
The Economics of the Transition Period (1920)
The New Course in Economic Policy (1921)
The Road to Socialism and the Worker-Peasant Alliance (1925)
The Theory of "Organised Economic Disorder" (1929)

". . . as this most interesting collection of his writings once again makes plain, outside the Soviet Union Bukharin's remains a name to be reckoned with: for better or worse, he was a main architect of modern communism, and thus, in unvarnished truth, one of the makers of the twentieth century."

Ken Coates

353 pages   ISBN 0 85124 275 8   Socialist Classics No.4

Pigs' Meat

Selected Writings of Thomas Spence
With an introductory essay and notes by G.I. Gallop

THOMAS SPENCE, Radical, land-reformer, dismissed schoolmaster and poverty-stricken book-pedlar, died at the age of 64 in 1814 "leaving nothing . . . but an injunction to promote his Plan and the remembrance of his inflexible integrity". Soon afterwards, the society which tried to preach his doctrines was banned by Act of Parliament.

In the story of the emergence of British radicalism and socialism in the late eighteenth and early nineteenth centuries, the works of Thomas Spence are an indispensable element. He produced a comprehensive argument for political and social revolution based on what he liked to call the "real" rights of man. Decentralisation, common ownership, participation and mutuality were central features of his ideas. We may indeed call him Britain's "first modern socialist".

This representative collection of his surviving writings, edited with a detailed introduction by G.I. Gallop, at last restores to the modern Labour movement a rich part of its partimony, long neglected and underestimated.

The selection includes:

The Rights of Man (1793)

The End of Oppression (1795)

A Letter from Ralph Hodge to his Cousin Thomas Bull (1795)

The Meridian Sun of Liberty (1796)

The Rights of Infants (1797)

The Restorer of Society to its Natural State (1803)

"Mr Gallop has done us a considerable service in making available a good and representative selection of Spence's writings."

A.L. Morton, *Morning Star*

192 pages   ISBN 0 85124 315 0   Socialist Classics No.2